"Oliver DeMille and Shanon Brooks have given insights into the Leadership Education model for teens that are not only easily understood but inspiring to read. Their teachings give credence to my voice as a parent using this model in my home. The Teen 100 Book List and the insights on how to use it are, of themselves, worth the price of the book!"

—Teri Helms, TJEd mom to 5 boys [www.tommymom.com]

"This book is so-o-o-o good. I am getting a copy for every single one of my young adult children for Christmas even though all but one are now in their 20s (17, 20, 23, 25, 26, 28). I'm buying a copy for every member of my family! The content is invaluable. I think this book is going to have a huge impact on the young people who read it."

— Deena Ortiz, Director of SoCal FATJEF TJEd Forum

"Every once in a while a second witness comes along and in one magical moment says something that speaks truth to the soul; and the person finally remembers who he is. That is what Oliver DeMille and Shanon Brooks have done. They remind us who we are and what we're about."

—Tiffany Earl, Author, *Say*Go*Be*Do*
Founder & Director LEMI Scholar Projects™
www.libercommunities.org

"This book will allow you, as a youth, to feel, to know, and to see how much we love you, how important you are to us, and why YOU ARE SO WORTH IT! Read it, apply it, live it, and enjoy being YOU!"

—Kami Mitchell, Director of Youth For Freedom (YFF)
Leadership Youth Conferences
www.youthforfreedom.org

Brilliant! A book on leadership written to the ultimate target audience, the leaders of the next generation! This book is not just a remake of TJEd; it's completely new material that really speaks to our current needs as parents and educators. Not only will I be recommending it to my students, but to their parents as well. What a gift to our teens, our nation and ourselves!

> — **Shawn Crane, Founder & Moderator**
> **TJEdMuse@yahoo.com**

"This a MUST READ for today's youth and their parents! Don't let the word TEENS in the title fool you. This book gives enormous perspective for all ages. We live in difficult times; our children have a big task ahead of them. DeMille and Brooks have prescribed usable, inspiring medicine for the maladies of our modern society and delivered them in a way everyone can understand."

> — **Nicholeen Peck, author of *Parenting A House United***
> **http://teachingselfgovernment.com**

"Whether a business plan, a personal schedule, or a wilderness trek plan, great ideas only have results when they are executed. That's the secret: execution, execution, execution. That's why this book is so valuable—it gives fun, practical, meaningful ideas and examples that focus on execution. We'll definitely be reading it at Williamsburg Academy."

> — **James C. Ure, Esq.**
> **Headmaster, Williamsburg Academy**

"I have read TJEd for Teens and loved the work. I definitely want to share this with my own teens and teens I mentor in my classrooms, both live and online. Talking straight to teens empowers them and they almost always rise to the occasion. Thank you for creating this work and speaking with such dignity to the youth."

> — **Donna Goff**
> **Co-Founder, The Princess Academies, LLC**

Thomas Jefferson Education

FOR

Teens

(And Every Adult Who Wants to Change the World)

Oliver DeMille

Shanon Brooks

THE LEADERSHIP EDUCATION LIBRARY

For information, email contact@TJEd.org.

This work is for informational purposes only; readers should consult competent professionals with questions regarding emotional, educational, medical and other concerns. Minors should complete the activities and exercises described in this book under the direction of a parent or guardian.

Published 2013 in the United States of America
Published by TJEd.org.

Cover and book design by Daniel Ruesch Design, Inc.

Library of Congress Control Number: 2013930733
ISBN 978-0-9830996-7-3

TJEd.org
February 2013

Contents

LEADERS ARE READERS.

TO

AMBER

OLIVER

JON

EMMA

SARA

GINNIE

BEN

ELIZA

DONYA

FREEBORN

SAMMY

HYRUM

AMERICA

AND

ABIGAIL

IT IS SAID THAT WHEN GOD WANTS TO CHANGE THE WORLD, HE SENDS A BABY—PERFECTLY TIMED TO GROW, LEARN, PREPARE AND THEN TAKE ACTION AT THE RIGHT MOMENT.

BUT THERE ARE TIMES WHEN ONE BABY WON'T SUFFICE, WHEN THE CHALLENGES FACING THE WORLD ARE JUST TOO GREAT; AND SO INSTEAD OF A GREAT REFORMER OR A FEW KEY THINKERS, WHAT IS NEEDED IS A WHOLE GENERATION OF LEADERS.

THIS HAPPENED IN THE SIXTH CENTURY B.C., AND IN THE FIRST DECADE OF THE COMMON ERA, THEN AGAIN IN THE AMERICAN FOUNDING GENERATION.

WE BELIEVE IT IS HAPPENING AGAIN TODAY...

1
YOUR FUTURE

A lot of books to young people in their teens seem to be just dumbed-down versions of the original. We think that's weird because it should be just the opposite. We believe today's youth are more sophisticated, involved and interested in world events and the future than the young people of most past generations. Some would say that they are also more intelligent than any generation in history. We tend to agree.

We believe this generation of youth is the most gifted and promising generation ever. So we intend to give you the deep stuff, the real treatment. We hope you will read *A Thomas Jefferson Education* in addition to this book—the two are totally different writings, and in our experience teens are up to the regular version as much as any adult. This book is written to tell the youth some additional, vital, deep things.

> "Happiness is the aim of life. Virtue is the foundation of happiness."
> *Thomas Jefferson*

We also want your parents and grandparents to read this book. Their generations are essential to what the world needs.

So let's get deep right now.

WHEN GOD WANTS TO CHANGE THE WORLD...

It is said that when God wants to change the world, he sends a baby—perfectly timed to grow, learn, prepare and then take action at the right moment. Whether you believe in God or the Universe, or whatever you want to call the powers higher than man, you can see how much sense this makes. We believe it is true: when God sees a need coming in the world, he sends a baby.

But there are times when one baby won't suffice, when the challenges the world faces are just too much; and so instead of a great reformer or a few key people, what is needed is a whole generation of leaders.

When the world is broken, a generation is born.

We live in such a world. And you are such a generation.

Gandhi is often credited with saying that you should *be* the change you wish to see in the world. We wonder if he meant literally that you should change the world's problems in yourself? Maybe. But we think he also meant that you should be who you were truly born to be—the best, true, Real You!

Is there anything in the world as powerful as a person who is truly himself? Or herself? Especially when the person is in love with good?

We don't think so.

That is what the teen years are all about—finding the Real You.

TEENAGER, GROWN UP OR ADULT?

If you don't find the Real You, you'll never really grow up. That is why there are a lot of immature people walking around, adults who have never quite figured out who they really are—so they just spend their lives making a living, seeking evening entertainment, wishing they were happy, sometimes seeming in control of their lives for a while but always eventually breaking down and wishing they could get it together.

You may not know it, but in truth many adults are that way. Why? Because they haven't yet figured out who they really are. We know that's a little scary, but we told you we'd give you the truth, the real deal. Here it is: You don't want to be like that when you are fifty, or thirty-eight, or even twenty-three years old. You want to be a true grown up when the time is right—not just an adult.

So it is vital that you figure out who you really are **now**, as a teen. That's what the teen years are for.

In this book, we're going to tell you how to do this. And we're going to help adults do the same.

We have questioned the use of the term "teenager" in the past. This is not because we have any negative thoughts toward your generation. In fact, it is just the opposite. We are so impressed with your generation and with you as individuals that we get frustrated when some people see your young age and don't expect much out of you.

So we've suggested on many occasions that parents avoid teaching their children to become "teenagers," which society sees as adolescents that behave like spoiled children. We believe that parents should expect a higher standard of youth who are capable of maturity and want to behave like adults.

In this book we are going to use "youth" and "teen" interchangeably. We're doing this with the more mature definition of "young adult" in mind. We are convinced that this is more in keeping with the real, genuine you.

The world today needs what your generation has to share! It needs you to be your real, best self! Those of us in the older generations need your generation to lead out in changing the world!

THE YOUTH LEAD THE WORLD

This may sound backwards at first. Shouldn't the older generations take the lead? Well, in theory, maybe. But in reality there are two truths that we all need to clearly understand if the world is going to improve:

1. The young are usually more idealistic and open to change than their elders.
2. Leadership comes more naturally to those who have had a chief hand in their own education.

These two powerful ideas go together, and the hidden secret in all this is that God/the Universe wants to educate the world! So he sends babies who become teens.

The future will be either a success or a failure, depending on whether or not today's youth can teach the world what they came here to teach it—before they forget who they are and just care about making a living.

That's deep.

And it's true.

Welcome to TJEd for Teens! Whether you are 13, 19, 39, or 99 this book is for anyone who wants a great education.

Now, your parents are your best friends in all of this. Other adults who understand your true potential are also great helps.

REALISM OR IDEALISM?

It always surprises us how some adults tell today's youth that you're a great generation and that you'll do amazing things, and then talk down to you like you're in kindergarten. The truth is that older generations have a lot of wisdom, but they seldom think to share it with you. You should listen to your parents and others who "get it" and who realize just how important you are.

The secret of success for today's youth is to differentiate between the wisdom of older generations and any overly pessimistic "realism."

Generations of youth that build on the wisdom of the past by adding their idealism and enthusiasm really can change the world for good! But generations where the young people ignore the wisdom of their elders or accept an inheritance of cynical "realism" and "*you-can't-do-it*-ism" fail to live up to their generational mission.

This may seem tricky, and in truth it is complex. You have to mix wisdom with idealism, enthusiasm with the rejection of most realism, and optimism with truly realistic choices. As we said, it's not as simple as many might think. In fact, just look at the kind of world the last four generations of youth have given us as they've grown up and taken charge. There is a lot that's good in the world—more than the nightly news ever admits—but the world also has a lot of problems. Fixing them is hard—*really hard!*—or it would have been done already.

THIS IS THE TIME

Some people see the teen years as a time to play, play, play and have as much fun as possible before taking on these problems; but in truth what could be better than using these years to prepare to fix the challenges of the world? Becoming what you were born to be can be fulfilling and a lot of fun. As we already said, your parents and other adults who understand this are your best friends. The key is for you to let them know where you stand. Sometimes you just want to have fun, and that is great—that's one of the blessings of being a teen. You can sometimes put fixing the world aside and just enjoy life.

Other times you really want to be thinking about and preparing for future leadership, for the time when you are changing the world as you were born to do. As a teen you get to move back and forth between these two.

To get the help and understanding you need, though, you need to let your parents know which of these things you are doing right now. It's okay to just tell them, "I want to be a kid now," and then later say, "Now I want to be an adult." Just be fine with them treating you differently, depending on which life stage you are living right now. They've been there, and they get it. But don't expect your parents to read your mind. Let them know when you want to be a kid, and be happy with them treating you that way. Let them know when you want to be an adult, and then act like it.

But just for the record: There are lots of things out there that cater to the kid in you; this book is written to the adult in you.

So many things in this world need to be fixed, and God/the Universe has sent many of this generation to do the fixing. You personally have a great role to play in this, and part of the teen years is finding out what that role is.

PREPARING FOR YOUR ROLE

Whatever your role, it will likely be hard. Here is the truth: only a truly great education will make you ready for the task! Without a truly superb education, very few people are able to figure out what they are supposed to know—how to always tell the difference between wisdom and pessimism, idealism and just being too naïve, and the true, excellent kind of proactive, innovative realism versus its counterfeits.

Great education is usually not formal so if you get a great education it will likely be in addition to school—not because of it. Don't get us wrong; schools have great tools for a superb education. It is just that most school "systems" don't allow you to use the tools optimally.

For example, most schools have libraries, but few allow or encourage students to spend most of their time in the library just reading and thinking. Most schools have some truly great teachers, but few students spend long hours discussing important ideas with these teachers in small groups and medium-size groups of other students—day after day, month after month. Bells, schedules, social cliques and administrative policies get in the way of the really great learning opportunities.

The great wisdom of mankind is found in the works of the greatest men and women who ever lived—from Socrates to Shakespeare, Gandhi to Mother Teresa, Nietzsche to Einstein, Moses to Christ, Buddha to Confucius, Picasso to Bach, Jane Austen to Abraham Lincoln, Martin Luther King, Jr. to Nikola Tesla, Agassiz and Thomas Jefferson, etc.

The list goes on and is thousands of names long. Their writing, composing, painting, equations and so many other works are full of ideas to discuss and argue with, experiments to duplicate and build from, equations to re-work and theories to improve upon—learning the best and worst of the past in order to gain true wisdom, knowledge and understanding. The youth of today are so ready to learn these truths.

Most schools resort to pre-digested textbooks instead of the original, inspiring classics. To get the great education you need, you don't want to settle for anything less than the best!

The overwhelmingly prevalent result of most schools is mediocre education, even at some of the most prestigious institutions. If you want great education, look for great classics, mentors and small group discussions—a lot of them! Find or found schools that emphasize lots of personal reading of the greats, individualized studies, which empower your personal goals and interests, and lots of personalized projects and writing. Look for mentors who will help you achieve your unique life mission by gaining the skills and knowledge you need to become the best you.

CONVEYOR BELT VS. GENIUS IN TRAINING

A mediocre education teaches mostly rote knowledge, while great education significantly develops your ability to think—really think—deeply, broadly, in the short and long terms, creatively and independently. Great education also teaches you to effectively write, speak in public, persuade, initiate, lead, influence and impact.

Conveyor-belt education convinces and trains people to "fit in" whereas Leadership Education helps you develop your natural genius to both follow and lead, alone and in teams.

Let's get one thing straight right now: there is *genius* in you! This is true. Your best teachers and mentors understand this without anyone telling them. A great education is all about finding your genius, finding who you really are and what you were born to do, and then developing your genius so you have the knowledge, skills and wisdom to be who you were born to be. If you think this doesn't apply to you, think again—because it does!

We don't mean by this that anybody is inherently better than anyone else, but that you are just as good as everybody else. You are. Your education is all about becoming the true, genuine, real, best you.

DOES PRESTIGE EQUAL QUALITY?

There is a problem in that some people too often confuse what education really is with the name on a school marquis. You'll encounter the sentiment that the most prestigious schools are the best schools, but that is not always true. The "right" schools for your mission are best, and it is your job to find them. Specifically, it is your role to find the best mentors, classics and studies for you—each at the right time in your life. If one of these happens to be prestigious too, that's great—as long as your criteria is *quality* and what is *right* for your mission.

In fact, if your mission does include time at a celebrated, high-status school, the best way to get your application accepted is to be able to converse freely about the great classical authors and their works, history, art, science, religion etc.—in interviews, on applications and in entrance essays.

And while we'll spend a lot of time here discussing how to get that kind of great preparation, we're not going to focus on institutions—rather we will emphasize great education.

The idea that prestigious schools are the best educators has a long history, but the truth is that graduates from the prestigious institutions simply make more money per capita than grads from other schools. So if your mission and purpose in going to school is to make a lot of money, aiming for prestige might help. But be honest with yourself, and understand that you'll only make money from these degrees if after graduation you spend a lot of your time on the process of making money. If you want to truly change the world, to improve it, your education must be ideal for you.

What About Financial Success?

Now, to be crystal clear, it may be that you were born to make a lot of money, that this is a vital part of your mission. If this is true, entrepreneurship is where the greatest wealth is created. Even those who don't find that formal schooling prepares them well for their mission still need a great education! In fact, the mentored, classical Leadership Education we're promoting here is the kind that many iconically successful entrepreneurs have pursued anyway.

If your mission in life is to be a professional—say, an attorney or a doctor—it may be that prestige is helpful to your mission and right to pursue. If so, nothing will better prepare you for this path later in life than a truly great education in your teens. Prestige schools love applicants with a superb education in the classics and a strong resume of service and achievement.

In short, whether your college and/or graduate school plans end up emphasizing getting more Leadership Education, generating wealth through entrepreneurship, being a great mother or father, engaging a professional career, being an educator, a community leader or something else, we can't think of a better way to prepare in your teen years (or later in life as an adult) than getting a quality, mentored education in the greatest classics of mankind!

That's what this book is all about.

THE FIRST STEP ON THE PATH TO GREATNESS

Whatever path you take later, nothing beats a truly great Leadership Education now. Leadership Education—the kind with classics, mentors, lots of discussion, simulations, writing, public speaking, leadership skills and so on—is the best preparation for life! We call this model TJEd, or the Seven Keys; but whatever you call it—get it!

As a teen, of course, you don't have to decide your whole life's path right now. You probably have someone who pays for your food, clothing and housing. If you do have a job, you probably don't have to spend your money on these basic necessities. Your job typically isn't sixty to eighty hours a week like many people on salary or even forty to fifty hours a week like many hourly wage workers. You probably aren't supporting your children who will suffer if you don't make enough.

Most likely you have a great luxury few adults have, something most adults would give almost anything for—you don't have to work most of the time in order to live so you have 8 to 15 hours a day of discretionary time. Even if you are in formal school and have a part-time job, you still have at least 15 hours a week to study. Most teens have three times that, or more!

"So what?" you might ask. Most adults will tell you that they wish they had extra time to read because they still want a truly great education now as adults.

Every generation has its idealists that hope to make the world a better place and solve all our problems for good. We hope that some generation will eventually figure it all out. It will take more than a few people here and there. Nearly every generation has an Einstein, a Hawking, a Churchill or a da Vinci. But it takes a lot more than a sole genius to really fix things. It takes a whole lot of us finding our genius, our best self, our real, genuine purpose in life and then doing it—even though it is hard.

Fifty Years From Now

Hey, by the time you are sixty everybody you know will have had a hard life—health problems, financial setbacks, consequences of dumb choices, marriage struggles, or something. Some people stay healthy and some build great marriages, but nobody is exempt from hardships. Life makes sure of that. So you might as well choose the noble path right now and set out to make the world better. It will be hard, but you'll end up really making a difference.

In about fifty years you will be old, no matter what. Will you just be old, or will you be old and victorious? Will you have done great things?

Two choices right now will make all the difference, whatever your age. The first is to really listen and follow the wisdom of the wise—whether they are parents, grandparents, church leaders, sages, or whoever. The second is to know how to recognize true wisdom, to separate it from all the other information and to use it well!

We need a generation of leaders, and you were born to be one. One requirement: you must have a great, not mediocre, truly superb education. That's what your teen years are for: figuring this all out and getting the education to prepare you for leadership. Or, if your teen years are past, *now* is the time to do this!

The truth is that as a teen nothing is as important as finding out who you really are, discovering what you are supposed to do with your life and then preparing for it! This book is about how to find and develop your genius identity while having fun at the same time.

Whatever your age, if you follow the advice in this book, you will greatly succeed in getting a superb Leadership Education! This will lay a commanding groundwork for whatever directions you take later. If you skip this opportunity to get a truly great education, you will miss out on one of the greatest chances of your lifetime.

THE GENIUS IN YOU

You have genius in you. We know it, and our purpose in writing this book is to help you find it. Your parents know it, and they want to help you find it and develop it. Others know you have genius and want to help too.

The future of the world depends on your generation finding its genius. Your personal future also depends on you finding it. This really matters.

You were born with a great mission and purpose in this life, just like Thomas Jefferson. Jefferson got a great, world-class Leadership Education in the classics during his teens, and then continued to build on it and use it to make a huge positive difference in the world—throughout his life. His influence is still being felt.

Your purpose is not to copy Thomas Jefferson or anyone else, but to do like he did—find *your* true inner genius, develop it, polish it to levels of greatness and then use it to help the world.

This will be a generational effort, so we hope you will read, discuss and share this book and these ideas with other teens and adults—a lot! The more teens in this generation who choose to get a great Leadership Education, the greater the future will be.

Now, let's start at the beginning. How can you get a truly superb, great, world-class Leadership Education?

2
CLASSICS

Perhaps you have heard of the Seven Keys of Great Teaching. They are the core of any truly quality education. Knowing them is exciting for at least two reasons: First, they turn most schooling upside down, showing you how to really learn. Second, billions of youth around the world right now desperately need to know them, and by familiarizing yourself with them, you'll get to share these incredibly powerful ideas!

Those who know the Seven Keys and use them will lead the world in thirty years. You get to help find and prepare these leaders by emailing, twittering, facebooking and getting the message out in every possible way!

Learn and use the Seven Keys, and you will find your true, genuine inner genius and become the leader you were born to be. Share these Keys with others and help them choose to use them, and you will be creating the future leaders all around the globe.

Like we said, these Keys are exciting!

"The field of imagination is thus laid open to our use and lessons may be formed to illustrate and carry home to the heart every moral rule of life. Thus the lively and lasting sense of filial duty is more effectually impressed upon the mind of a son or daughter by reading King Lear, than by all the dry volumes of ethics and divinity that were ever written. This is my idea of well written Romance, of Tragedy, Comedy, and Epic poetry."

Thomas Jefferson

Your Best Mentors and Greatest Allies

Before we get into this powerful, secret information, let's talk about how vital it is to include your parents in your learning. (By the way, this information is secret because so few people in the world know the Seven Keys, not because it is hidden in any way; we all need to share these secrets far and wide.) Your parents (or in some cases your guardians) are your true mentors, and their thoughts are way more important for you than ours. You should run everything you learn by them, and get their permission to apply anything in this book. We mean it!

We're giving general information here, and we don't know you or your specific situation at all. They know you very well, and if they disagree with us on any or all of what is written here, listen to them first and follow their advice. Your relationship with them and trust in them is much more important than anything we say in this book.

In fact, we highly recommend that, wherever possible, you discuss each chapter of this book with a group that includes your parents and also other youth.

Now, let's look at seven of the most powerful secrets and true principles in the world! Learn them. Memorize them. Apply them every day. Share them far and wide, especially with other teens.

The Seven Keys Of Great Teaching

The Seven Keys of Great Teaching will change the world if you learn them, use them and share them. Here they are:

1. Classics, not textbooks
2. Mentors, not professors
3. Inspire, not require
4. Structure time, not content
5. Quality, not conformity
6. Simple, not complex
7. You, not them

We will learn a little about each of them in this chapter and the following chapters.

Classics, Not Textbooks

Why would you study dumbed-down versions of things when you can learn face to face with greatness from the best thinkers and leaders on any topic from all human history?

For example, you can learn strategy from Caesar, Napoleon, De Saxe and Jomini. Learn art and art history from Michelangelo, Rembrandt, Picasso and Van Gogh and composition from Beethoven, Bach, Mozart, Copland and even Clapton. Really! Great education comes from great artists, historians, authors, statesmen, scientists, prophets and a variety of religious thinkers, philosophers and leaders, etc.

Learn science directly from Newton, Einstein and Hawking. Sure, use a textbook for reference and to work problems; but emphasize the greats—Archimedes, Euclid and so many others. When you study with the greats, you learn not just *how* to do math or science; you resonate with the questions that inspired their advances and learn the *Why*. This is key. The Why is the spice, the flavor and the excitement.

Read about government directly from Tocqueville's *Democracy in America*, Madison's *Federalist Papers* or the writings of Jefferson.

Study statesmanship from Lincoln's own words, and Churchill's, Gandhi's and Margaret Thatcher's. Learn citizenship from Rosa Parks and the writings of George Washington and so many others. Learn public speaking from the examples of Pericles, Joan of Arc, Luther, John Adams, JFK, Martin Luther King, Jr., Ronald Reagan, Obama, etc.

Straight From The Original Sources

Classics are the most exciting way to study. Learn great writing from *Pride and Prejudice, Les Miserables,* Shakespeare and from the other greatest writers and writings in history. Learn poetry directly from Milton and about Islam directly from the Qur'an. Study communism directly from Marx, Lenin and Solzhenitsyn and freedom in the writings of Benjamin Franklin, Andrew Jackson, Frederic Bastiat and so many others.

Learn history the exciting way—from the biographies of the greatest men and women in history. Don't forget to include the worst, like Hitler, Stalin and Mao. The list of topics and classics just goes on and on.

This is what a great education is! Know what the greatest leaders of history knew and what today's greatest leaders know—from the same place they got it: the greatest classics. Classics have the very best and worst and most influential ideas, thoughts, people, creations, documents and events of all humanity—that's why they are "the classics." Add to these the great religious works of the world, and the most important works from your own belief system, and you have the basics of a truly great education.

THINK WHAT, AND HOW, THEY THOUGHT

Not only are the contents of classics the best, but by studying the greatest minds of mankind you learn to think at their level! Run the ideas and thoughts presented in these classics by your parents and other adults that care about you. Discuss, consider, analyze and compare. Don't just sponge everything you read; question, ponder and debate. Challenge the ideas that are flawed or poorly reasoned; consider how you can improve on them. Embrace and apply the ideas and principles that improve on *you*. Find out what your parents and other mentors think about what you've read. Benefit from their insights and viewpoints as well.

When you know the things that are best learned in the classics, you have a foundation upon which to compare, consider, analyze and choose at the level of world-class leadership. This is how the wealthy classes are educated in every generation. Likewise, those with classic-based education can achieve their life mission on the same level as the wealthy classes. Without a classic-based education, you just don't know the secrets the educated wealthy know, and you will be forever relegated to the level that lesser-privileged classes have protested with relative futility for centuries.

Introducing: "The List"

In this next section we will introduce The Teen 100 Book List. The people in leadership in governments and businesses around the world are largely familiar with most of these works and nearly all the ideas they teach. It is not an exaggeration to say that the ideas in these works are the difference between the rich/powerful/leaders and the poor/weak/masses.

These classics are full of potent, "secret" information that has been used for centuries to run, move and impact the world. Only a very small portion of the population of the world has read all these books—certainly less than 1%! Knowledge of the greatest ideas and events is the starting point of a great education, and it is vital to leadership preparation.

Rather than just give you a list of book titles and authors (how many times have you seen that before?) we're first going to give you an outline for how to best study and learn from this list.

First, go through the following list and put a dot next to those you have already read. Really. Do that now. (Then come back to this place.)

There, wasn't that cool? Whether you've marked a bunch of them, or seen a bunch of titles that you've been meaning to get to (or both), now you have a flavor of what's to come. But again: we have specific suggestions on how to go about this.

There are three levels to your study. With some books you will choose to only do one level and on others two levels. With those you really want to learn in Depth, do all three levels.

Level One: Break the Taboo

Level One is to read the book and take notes in it. Yes, **write *in*** the book! (Of course, this only applies if you own it.) Get your parents' permission if you are using their book; maybe it will help a little if you tell them that we recommend it. ;-)

Our kids LOVE studying from the books that have our notes in them, and we love seeing their additions when their own comments have been added to ours. Some of our most prized possessions are volumes that our mentors have studied in years past which have their personal notations in the margins and end pages.

Yes, we know that one of the first lessons you were taught was that "books are our friends." Don't tear the pages, don't eat on them, and for heavens' sake **Don't Write In Them!**

That was a good rule for when you were a toddler. But now—get over the taboo of writing in a book! How else are you going to have a conversation with a dead writer? Or with other readers who pick up the volume years apart from each other? Or with yourself, when taking it up again? Taking notes in the book allows you to come back to it later and remember details much more quickly and easily than otherwise.

If you don't own the book, take notes in a notebook; you can sometimes use one notebook for several books. (You can find recommendations for a cataloguing system for these notes at www.TJEdforTeens.com) Of course, never deface or write in a library book or one owned by someone else. But this brings us to an important aside: We highly encourage you to begin building your own library now. Buy as many of the Teen 100 Book List as you can over time. These books will become your friends and the notes you write in them will become invaluable to you over time.

While taking notes, write whatever comes to mind, such as:

☞ things you agree with

☞ things you disagree with

☞ questions that arise in your mind

☞ words you don't know (look them up and write the definitions)

☞ examples of excellent writing

☞ selections you want to memorize

☛ dates or facts you want to remember

☛ other things that come to you which seem important

When you have read the book and taken notes about it or in it, check it off the list by marking Level One. (That's right; write in *THIS* book.)

LEVEL TWO: TALK IT OVER

Level Two occurs when you have read a book, taken notes, and then participated in a discussion about the book with at least one other person. Discussion can be in person, online or in writing, and can be with one other person or a group. In all things online, of course, follow wise safety guidelines. If you don't have any, discuss and make a list of rules with your parents. It is a good idea to never share your details about your contact information, your family's identity, etc. Be really open to having your parents review your communications with others online. They will be able to point out to you situations or people that you might not realize could be a problem. Besides, what you do online reflects on them and impacts the safety even of your younger siblings. You can benefit from your parents' input on how to be safe and appropriate online.

The TJEd Discussion Group on Facebook [www.facebook.com/groups/tjeddiscussion] and the TJEd MUSE email group [www.groups.yahoo.com/group/tjedmuse] are great ways to interact about books and other topics of interest with others on the path of Leadership Education. Completing Level Two will likely multiply and expand your memory of the details and ideas in the book you discuss. This isn't based on scientific research, but on our experience and the stories of hundreds of students. Almost everyone who discusses a book with others learns and also remembers a lot more. Hearing the views of others on what you have read really broadens and deepens your learning experience. When you are younger and/or just starting this process, parents and those close to you are a great place to start.

Each time you complete a book discussion, tick off that bubble on the list!

Level Three: Teach to Learn

This level increases your learning even more—a lot more! In Level Three you write a paper or outline on the key ideas from the book and then teach it to others. In our informal testing of this technique we've discovered that those who teach are able to learn and remember an average of 80% more than those who don't. Teaching is a powerful learning method—whether through oral presentation or through persuasive writing. As the old saying goes, the teacher always learns more than the student.

A visitor to our classrooms several years ago was so impressed with how much the students were learning that he enrolled as a student for a semester just to figure out how they did it. He was a professional teacher with a long career in education, and he was simply amazed at the quality and quantity of our students' learning.

After watching every class period closely for a semester, he told Oliver that he had figured out our secret. *"You make every student the teacher,"* he said, *"not by putting them in front of a class but by having them do everything a teacher would do to prepare to teach each class and then letting them actually participate in the teaching."*

Try this yourself to see just how much it improves your learning. If you ask adults what they remember most from college classes, most will refer to papers they wrote or projects/reports they completed. People remember the things they've taught or presented much more than things they heard in lectures or memorized for exams.

Stand and Deliver

Interestingly, the exception to this is where students did oral exams—but this further makes the point! People remember things they taught, and oral exams are just a form of teaching. Multiple-choice tests are not. Many (if not most) teachers don't even look at them closely—they just record the scores. Next to oral exams, people remember essay questions they answered best. Actually teaching a class or writing an article is by far the best way to increase the relatable learning and also long-term memory of things studied.

Another benefit to learning in Level Three is that it usually requires us to re-read part or much of the book! This is incredibly powerful in the learning process, especially if we read through the notes we took and the areas we highlighted, underlined, circled or marked with "**!!!**".

100 + 40

The Teen 100 Book List is great reading for your teen years. Classics are numbered 1-100. Some of the books on the classic list are included to help teach special skills of language, mathematics, science, leadership, etc. and are numbered along with the literary classics.

In addition to the hundred classics, there are more than forty other books (note that some of the listings are series) that we consider to be helpful and even vital to a superb education because they inspire thinking. Each of these extras is marked with a ♥ to indicate "inspiring."

Of course, you can read things that aren't on the list and apply all three levels to them as well. But by reading this list and completing it all before you are eighteen or enroll full time in college, you'll be very well read in the leadership classics and well prepared for college or other leadership studies. This will greatly prepare you for whatever paths you choose after your teen years. You will have an excellent base of great reading in the most powerful ideas in the world!

The Teen 100 List is designed to precede the Adult/College Great 100 List found in *A Thomas Jefferson Education*. Very few titles are on both lists; the exceptions include authors such as Shakespeare on purpose, because they deserve multiple readings throughout the rest of your life.

For now, as you go through the list remember to:

☞ Mark all you have done, noting completion of each level

☞ Get started reading from the list

☞ Eventually read the entire list

As you go, do Level One on all books and Levels Two and Three according to your level of interest in each book. Ideally, you will do at least 130 at Level One, at least 75 at Level Two, and at least 40 at Level Three.

CLASSICAL LANGUAGES: MATH, LATIN, ETC.

On the study of mathematics, you will note that the recommendation is to study both great math classics and math workbooks. On the study of language, it is recommended to study Latin and one modern international language during the teen years, and ancient Hebrew with a second modern international language during the college years. Of course, this should be personalized to each student's needs. Latin is the language of the professions and Hebrew the language of freedom. Your own native tongue is, of course, a most important area of language study—especially in the great classics.

As you learn additional techniques in later chapters, add them to your studies of these great books on this list.

Are you ready to begin? You already made a mark by the titles you've previously read. Now, glance through the list one more time. This time put a special mark by any which particularly interest you right now. Once you have reviewed the entire list, pick a book or three and start *studying*!

THE TEEN 100 BOOK LIST!

AGE 13

(ages are just a general guideline; if possible, everyone should read the entire list for all ages)

1 Girls: Montgomery, *Anne of Green Gables*
    ○ Level One   ○ Level Two   ○ Level Three

1 Boys: Card, *Ender's Game*
    ○ Level One   ○ Level Two   ○ Level Three

2 Girls: Alcott, *Little Women*
    ○ Level One   ○ Level Two   ○ Level Three

2 Boys: Sanderson, *Elantris*
    ○ Level One   ○ Level Two   ○ Level Three

3 Movie: *Pride and Prejudice* (A&E Version)
    ○ Level One   ○ Level Two   ○ Level Three

4 Baum, *The Wizard of Oz*
    ○ Level One   ○ Level Two   ○ Level Three

5 Lewis, *The Lion, The Witch and the Wardrobe*
    ○ Level One   ○ Level Two   ○ Level Three

6 Hamilton, *Mythology*
    ○ Level One   ○ Level Two   ○ Level Three

7 Wilder, *Little House in the Big Woods*
    ○ Level One   ○ Level Two   ○ Level Three

8 Beginning Latin book (We have purposely left the Latin and Math books open for student and parent choice, but note that there are several good online sources as well as books. See www.TJEd.org and www.TJEdforTeens.com for further suggestions.)
    ○ Level One   ○ Level Two   ○ Level Three

9 Juster, *The Phantom Toll Booth*

    ◯ Level One   ◯ Level Two   ◯ Level Three

10 Arithmetic book (with problems to work; note that we have purposely left the math titles open, but you can find good mathematics resources at www.TJEd.org and www.TJEdforTeens.com)

    ◯ Level One   ◯ Level Two   ◯ Level Three

AGE 14

(ages are just a general guideline; if possible, everyone should read the entire list for all ages)

11 Porter, *Pollyanna*

    ◯ Level One   ◯ Level Two   ◯ Level Three

12 Shakespeare, *A Midsummer Night's Dream*

    ◯ Level One   ◯ Level Two   ◯ Level Three

13 Shakespeare, *All's Well That Ends Well*

    ◯ Level One   ◯ Level Two   ◯ Level Three

14 Shakespeare, *The Tempest*

    ◯ Level One   ◯ Level Two   ◯ Level Three

15 Lewis, *Prince Caspian*

    ◯ Level One   ◯ Level Two   ◯ Level Three

16 *Aesop's Fables*

    ◯ Level One   ◯ Level Two   ◯ Level Three

17 Twain, *Tom Sawyer*

    ◯ Level One   ◯ Level Two   ◯ Level Three

18 Beginning Latin book

    ◯ Level One   ◯ Level Two   ◯ Level Three

19 Abbott, *Flatland*

    ◯ Level One   ◯ Level Two   ◯ Level Three

20 Pre-Algebra book (with problems to work)

    ○ Level One   ○ Level Two   ○ Level Three

21 Twain, *Saint Joan*

    ○ Level One   ○ Level Two   ○ Level Three

22 Twain, *Huckleberry Finn*

    ○ Level One   ○ Level Two   ○ Level Three

23 Wilder, *Little House on the Prairie*

    ○ Level One   ○ Level Two   ○ Level Three

24 Felleman and Allen, *Best Loved Poems of the American People*

    ○ Level One   ○ Level Two   ○ Level Three

25 Shakespeare, Sonnets

    ○ Level One   ○ Level Two   ○ Level Three

26 Kipling, *The Jungle Book*

    ○ Level One   ○ Level Two   ○ Level Three

27 Allison, et. al., *The Real Thomas Jefferson*

    ○ Level One   ○ Level Two   ○ Level Three

28 Beginning Latin Primer

    ○ Level One   ○ Level Two   ○ Level Three

29 Asimov, *On Numbers*

    ○ Level One   ○ Level Two   ○ Level Three

30 Algebra I book (with problems to work)

    ○ Level One   ○ Level Two   ○ Level Three

Inspiring Supplements For Everyone

♥ DeMille and Brooks, *Thomas Jefferson Education for Teens*

    ○ Level One   ○ Level Two   ○ Level Three

♥ Covey, *The 7 Habits of Highly Effective Teens*

    ○ Level One   ○ Level Two   ○ Level Three

♥ Chapman, *The Five Love Languages of Teenagers*
   ○ Level One   ○ Level Two   ○ Level Three

♥ Strauss & Howe, *The Fourth Turning*
   ○ Level One   ○ Level Two   ○ Level Three

♥ L'Amour, *The Walking Drum*
   ○ Level One   ○ Level Two   ○ Level Three

♥ Earl, *Say*Go*Be*Do*
   ○ Level One   ○ Level Two   ○ Level Three

♥ Johnson and Blanchard, *The One Minute Manager*
   ○ Level One   ○ Level Two   ○ Level Three

♥ Kiyosaki, *The Cashflow Quadrant*
   ○ Level One   ○ Level Two   ○ Level Three

♥ Pink, *A Whole New Mind*
   ○ Level One   ○ Level Two   ○ Level Three

♥ DeMille, *Leadership Education*
   ○ Level One   ○ Level Two   ○ Level Three

♥ Bendick, *Archimedes and the Door of Science*
   ○ Level One   ○ Level Two   ○ Level Three

Other books each student should have include a good dictionary, a good thesaurus, a good Latin-English dictionary, *The Dictionary of Cultural Literacy* (Hirsch), *The Elements of Grammar* (Shertzer) and *The Timetables of History* (Grun and Simpson).

AGE 15

(ages are just a general guideline; if possible, everyone should read the entire list for all ages)

31 *The Declaration of Independence*
   ○ Level One   ○ Level Two   ○ Level Three

32 *The Constitution of the United States*
    ○ Level One   ○ Level Two   ○ Level Three

33 Skousen, *The Making of America*
    ○ Level One   ○ Level Two   ○ Level Three

34 Allison, et al, *The Real Benjamin Franklin*
    ○ Level One   ○ Level Two   ○ Level Three

35 Boom, *The Hiding Place*
    ○ Level One   ○ Level Two   ○ Level Three

36 Sophocles, *Antigone*
    ○ Level One   ○ Level Two   ○ Level Three

37 Parry, et al, *The Real George Washington*
    ○ Level One   ○ Level Two   ○ Level Three

38 Intermediate Latin book
    ○ Level One   ○ Level Two   ○ Level Three

39 Whitehead, *Introduction to Mathematics*
    ○ Level One   ○ Level Two   ○ Level Three

40 Algebra I book, continued (with problems to work)
    ○ Level One   ○ Level Two   ○ Level Three

41 Shakespeare, *Romeo and Juliet*
    ○ Level One   ○ Level Two   ○ Level Three

42 *The Monroe Doctrine*
    ○ Level One   ○ Level Two   ○ Level Three

43 Lincoln, "The Gettysburg Address"
    ○ Level One   ○ Level Two   ○ Level Three

44 Bastiat, *The Law*
    ○ Level One   ○ Level Two   ○ Level Three

45 Cooper, *The Deerslayer*
    ○ Level One   ○ Level Two   ○ Level Three

46 Orwell, *Animal Farm*

    ○ Level One   ○ Level Two   ○ Level Three

47 Homer, *Iliad*

    ○ Level One   ○ Level Two   ○ Level Three

48 Intermediate Latin book, continued

    ○ Level One   ○ Level Two   ○ Level Three

49 Schneider, *A Beginner's Guide to Constructing the Universe*

    ○ Level One   ○ Level Two   ○ Level Three

50 Geometry book (with proofs to work)

    ○ Level One   ○ Level Two   ○ Level Three

Inspiring Books To Supplement 100 List

♥ Woodward, *Resolved*

    ○ Level One   ○ Level Two   ○ Level Three

♥ Naisbitt, *Megatrends*

    ○ Level One   ○ Level Two   ○ Level Three

♥ Owen, *Here There Be Dragons*

    ○ Level One   ○ Level Two   ○ Level Three

♥ Bolon, *Cash, Cars and College*

    ○ Level One   ○ Level Two   ○ Level Three

♥ Eddings, *The Belgariad*

    ○ Level One   ○ Level Two   ○ Level Three

♥ Covey, *The 7 Habits of Highly Effective People*

    ○ Level One   ○ Level Two   ○ Level Three

♥ DeMille, *A Thomas Jefferson Education*

    ○ Level One   ○ Level Two   ○ Level Three

♥ Covey, et al., *First Things First*

    ○ Level One   ○ Level Two   ○ Level Three

❤ Strauss & Howe, *The Millennials*
   ○ Level One   ○ Level Two   ○ Level Three
❤ L'Amour, *Bendigo Shafter*
   ○ Level One   ○ Level Two   ○ Level Three
❤ Allen, *As A Man Thinketh*
   ○ Level One   ○ Level Two   ○ Level Three

Each student should also study SAT/ACT preparation books when the time is right.

AGE 16

(ages are just a general guideline; if possible, everyone should read the entire list for all ages)

51 Homer, *Odyssey*
   ○ Level One   ○ Level Two   ○ Level Three
52 Plato, *The Trial and Death of Socrates* (in four dialogues)
   ○ Level One   ○ Level Two   ○ Level Three
53 Austen, *Emma*
   ○ Level One   ○ Level Two   ○ Level Three
54 Shakespeare, *Hamlet*
   ○ Level One   ○ Level Two   ○ Level Three
55 *Torah, Genesis*
   ○ Level One   ○ Level Two   ○ Level Three
56 *Bible, Matthew*
   ○ Level One   ○ Level Two   ○ Level Three
57 *Qur'an, Cows*
   ○ Level One   ○ Level Two   ○ Level Three
58 Intermediate Latin Primer
   ○ Level One   ○ Level Two   ○ Level Three

59 Euclid, *Elements* books I-II

   ○ Level One   ○ Level Two   ○ Level Three

60 Algebra II book (with problems to work)

   ○ Level One   ○ Level Two   ○ Level Three

61 Sargent, *Our Home*

   ○ Level One   ○ Level Two   ○ Level Three

62 Twain, *A Connecticut Yankee in King Arthur's Court*

   ○ Level One   ○ Level Two   ○ Level Three

63 King, "I Have a Dream"

   ○ Level One   ○ Level Two   ○ Level Three

64 Hugo, *Les Miserables*

   ○ Level One   ○ Level Two   ○ Level Three

65 Tocqueville, *Democracy in America*

   ○ Level One   ○ Level Two   ○ Level Three

66 Da Vinci, *Notebooks*

   ○ Level One   ○ Level Two   ○ Level Three

67 Douglass, *Narrative of the Life of Frederick Douglass*

   ○ Level One   ○ Level Two   ○ Level Three

68 Advanced Latin book

   ○ Level One   ○ Level Two   ○ Level Three

69 Nichomachus, *Arithmetic*

   ○ Level One ○ Level Two ○ Level Three

70 Algebra II book, continued (with problems to work)

   ○ Level One   ○ Level Two   ○ Level Three

71 Wattles, *The Science of Getting Rich*

   ○ Level One   ○ Level Two   ○ Level Three

72 Henry, "Give Me Liberty or Give Me Death"

   ○ Level One   ○ Level Two   ○ Level Three

73 Shakespeare, *Othello*

○ Level One ○ Level Two ○ Level Three

74 McCrae, *In Flanders Field*

○ Level One ○ Level Two ○ Level Three

75 Austen, *Pride and Prejudice*

○ Level One ○ Level Two ○ Level Three

76 Tzu, *The Art of War*

○ Level One ○ Level Two ○ Level Three

Inspiring Supplements

♥ Brady, *Rascal*

○ Level One ○ Level Two ○ Level Three

♥ Gatto, *Dumbing Us Down*

○ Level One ○ Level Two ○ Level Three

♥ Eddings, *The Mallorean*

○ Level One ○ Level Two ○ Level Three

♥ Householder, *The Jackrabbit Factor*

○ Level One ○ Level Two ○ Level Three

♥ DeMille, *The Coming Aristocracy*

○ Level One ○ Level Two ○ Level Three

♥ Girls: Eldridge, *Wild at Heart*

○ Level One ○ Level Two ○ Level Three

♥ Boys: Eldridge, *Captivating*

○ Level One ○ Level Two ○ Level Three

♥ DeMille and Jeppson, *The Thomas Jefferson Education Home Companion*

○ Level One ○ Level Two ○ Level Three

♥ Chapman, *The Five Love Languages*
    O Level One   O Level Two   O Level Three

♥ Covey, *The Eighth Habit*
    O Level One   O Level Two   O Level Three

♥ DeMille and Earl, *The Student Whisperer*
    O Level One   O Level Two   O Level Three

♥ DeMille, *1913*
    O Level One   O Level Two   O Level Three

♥ Coelho, *The Alchemist*
    O Level One   O Level Two   O Level Three

AGE 17-18

(ages are just a general guideline; if possible, everyone should read the entire list for all ages)

77 Buchanan, *Poetry and Mathematics*
    O Level One   O Level Two   O Level Three

78 Advanced Latin book
    O Level One   O Level Two   O Level Three

79 Euclid, *Elements* books III-IV
    O Level One   O Level Two   O Level Three

80 Trigonometry book (with problems to work)
    O Level One   O Level Two   O Level Three

81 Tolkien, *The Lord of the Rings* trilogy
    O Level One   O Level Two   O Level Three

82 Asimov, *The Foundation* series
    O Level One   O Level Two   O Level Three

83 Rawls, *Where the Red Fern Grows*
    O Level One   O Level Two   O Level Three

84 Moody, *Man of the Family*

    ○ Level One   ○ Level Two   ○ Level Three

85 Skousen, *The Five Thousand Year Leap*

    ○ Level One   ○ Level Two   ○ Level Three

86 Trigonometry Book, continued (with problems to work)

    ○ Level One   ○ Level Two   ○ Level Three

87 Lowell, "The Present Crisis"

    ○ Level One   ○ Level Two   ○ Level Three

88 Advanced Latin Book

    ○ Level One   ○ Level Two   ○ Level Three

89 Hawking, *A Brief History of Time*

    ○ Level One   ○ Level Two   ○ Level Three

90 Calculus book (with problems to work)

    ○ Level One   ○ Level Two   ○ Level Three

91 Girls: Card, *Ender's Game*

    ○ Level One   ○ Level Two   ○ Level Three

91 Boys: Alcott, *Little Women*

    ○ Level One   ○ Level Two   ○ Level Three

92 Girls: Sanderson, *Elantris*

    ○ Level One   ○ Level Two   ○ Level Three

92 Boys: Montgomery, *Anne of Green Gables*

    ○ Level One   ○ Level Two   ○ Level Three

93 Alcott, *Jo's Boys*

    ○ Level One   ○ Level Two   ○ Level Three

94 Alcott, *Little Men*

    ○ Level One   ○ Level Two   ○ Level Three

95 *The Dhammapada*

    ○ Level One   ○ Level Two   ○ Level Three

96 *The Bhagavad Gita*

    O Level One   O Level Two   O Level Three

97 Aristotle, *Nichomachaean Ethics*

    O Level One   O Level Two   O Level Three

98 Legal and Medical Latin book

    O Level One   O Level Two   O Level Three

99 Einstein, *Relativity*

    O Level One   O Level Two   O Level Three

100 Calculus book (with problems to work)

    O Level One   O Level Two   O Level Three

These books are so much fun! They are interesting, deep, fascinating, profound and powerful. We hope you really enjoy them! Go slow, discuss them a lot with others, and have fun learning from among the truly greatest writers and thinkers of all time.

3
MENTORS

Mentors make all the difference. The word "mentor" comes from The Odyssey, where the hero Odysseus must leave home for many years and leaves the teaching, guidance and care of his son Telemachus in the hands of a man he trusts to handle this responsibility well. The man's name is Mentor.

Imagine how much trust it would take to turn over such guidance to someone. Mentor was more than a teacher, more than a friend, more than a guide—he was basically another father. In a similar way, a college where one studies and graduates is known as the *alma mater*, which means the "mother of the soul." Most of us have a physical mother who guides and teaches us; then when we leave home to get a college education that learning becomes in a very real sense a second mother of our soul, and the mentor who facilitates that learning, a second father.

"When I recollect that at fourteen years of age, the whole care and direction of myself was thrown on myself entirely, without a relation or friend qualified to advise or guide me ... I am astonished I did not ... become ... worthless to society .... I had the good fortune to become acquainted very early with some characters of very high standing, and to feel the incessant wish that I could ever become what they were. Under temptations and difficulties, I would ask myself what would Dr. Small, Mr. Wythe, Peyton Randolph do in this situation?"

Thomas Jefferson

Going It Alone

Mentors make all the difference in how effective we are in almost every aspect of life. For example, imagine trying to learn karate without a mentor. You dress in the right clothes, get out a floor mat, and practice a lot in front of a mirror, day after day. But somehow—even as your moves become faster and more menacing—you just don't seem to get very good at self-defense! Not surprising, right? Of course you need a mentor who already knows karate.

Imagine that one day a black-belted instructor walks into the room where you are practicing. He shows you some moves and teaches you several key ideas. Within an hour you'll probably progress more than all the long hours of self-directed practice you already did. He gives you several things to work on. Now your self-practice time becomes a lot more useful. *That's the power of mentoring.*

Of course, it can be taken too far. Imagine that this instructor just lectures to you for 5-6 hours every day, then sends you home to practice an hour each night. You will learn, but not nearly as well as if he teaches you a couple of times a week for an hour and then expects you to practice what he has taught for long hours each week while apart from him.

This is how mentoring works. And it does work!

Trusting a Guide

Consider this idea as taught by John Assaraf and Murray Smith in their book *The Answer*: If a person unfamiliar with the Rubik's Cube were given one, blindfolded and told to solve the Cube alone, it is estimated that it would take over a million years to do it! But if a person who knows how to do the Rubik's Cube guides the blindfolded person with verbal commands, he can do it *in less than five minutes.*

Mentoring makes all the difference! Mentoring helps us progress more effectively and rapidly in learning skills like karate, music, ancient or foreign languages, the fine arts, writing, public speaking and much more. Mentors can help us in just about everything in life. They are especially helpful in getting a great education.

Actually, in the last chapter we talked a lot about one kind of mentor: authors of great works. When we read Einstein or Aristotle or Shakespeare, they mentor us with their ideas, wisdom, stories and thoughts. Great books even mentor us by their flaws or weaknesses.

WHO ARE YOUR MENTORS?

Some of our greatest mentoring can also come from the characters in books. For example, you may have been mentored by Elizabeth Bennett or Mr. Darcy in *Pride and Prejudice,* by Anne in *Anne of Green Gables,* or by Aragorn in *The Lord of the Rings.* Or you may have received mentoring from Ender or Bean in the Ender's Game series. Think of your favorite book or movie, and then ponder which of the characters mentored you most.

Yoda? Laura Ingalls? Jo? Captain Picard? Most books and movies can mentor us if we ponder and learn the lessons they offer.

Your friends are also natural mentors—as are leaders in places like school, scouts, church, youth conferences, and many other settings. And of course certain experiences in life teach deep mentor lessons.

There are many types of mentors that make all the difference in the quality of your teen education. Some are vital!

First, parent mentors are the most important mentors during your youth. They really are. Unfortunately, few teens take enough responsibility for the quality of that relationship and really take advantage of all the great benefits parents can offer as mentors.

MAKE IT EASY ON THEM

Parents are often very busy balancing career and family and community and finances and everything else in life. You can help them mentor you by not waiting around for them to do it all. Maybe you are lucky enough to have a parent who gives you lots of positive attention, guides effectively without manipulating and has plenty of time and energy to help you with all your needs and wants, always setting the right example, always smiling and calmly serving you. (We wish our kids had such fathers.) But maybe, more likely, you don't—at least not all the time.

But you almost certainly have a parent who truly loves you, who wants the very best for you and who really does want to help you. Not everybody is lucky enough to have one or two such parents, but the very fact that you're reading this book means you're probably in that group. If not, you can find other mentors to help.

To help your parents/mentors be even better mentors, try the following (by the way, this works for people of all ages, even is your parents have passed on):

- ☞ Thank God/the Universe that you are so lucky! Gratitude seems to have a way of bringing additional positives into your life.

- ☞ Tell (and/or show) your parents or closest guardians how much you love them. Love also brings more positives, especially when it is openly expressed.

- ☞ Thank them for specific things they do for you—right now, and often.

- ☞ Trust them—really, truly. Empower them to be their best by showing them your appreciation, trust and confidence even when they mess up.

- ☞ Forgive them. They are not perfect—nobody is—and they are probably the first to admit this. Just forgive them even if you aren't sure what you are forgiving them for. They struggle in life like everyone else, they love you and they are doing their best.

BREAK THE TABOO, II

Now, sit down and do the rest of this in writing. First, make a list of their greatest strengths. Ponder this and write at least 10 strengths per parent. (By the way, this is a great chance to Break the Taboo and start writing key ideas in your books as you study.)

First Parent/Mentor:

1 _____

2 _____

3 _____

4 _____

5 _____

6 _____

7 _____

8 _____

9 _____

10 _____

11 _____

12 _____

13 _____

Now go even deeper. What are his/her biggest dreams?

1 _____

2 _____

3 _____

4 _____

5 _____

Second Parent/Mentor:

1. _____
2. _____
3. _____
4. _____
5. _____
6. _____
7. _____
8. _____
9. _____
10. _____
11. _____
12. _____
13. _____

What are his/her biggest dreams?

1. _____
2. _____
3. _____
4. _____
5. _____

If you didn't take the time to answer all these, go back and do them.
It will really help. As you complete these, you are doing something

really important—you are thinking like a mentor! This helps you be a much better student.

The first role of mentors is to see genius in their students, and these lists help you see genius in yourself and others.

Now, list your greatest strengths. Don't be shy or falsely humble. You have strengths; list some of them below:

1 _____

2 _____

3 _____

4 _____

5 _____

6 _____

7 _____

Really ponder this and list your strengths.

Now, one more thing. This will greatly help you as well as your parents/mentors do the first step of mentoring. Don't overthink this. Just trust your gut and the first thoughts that come to your mind. What is your real genius? Write whatever comes to mind, even if it surprises you. Don't analyze or debate it, just write:

1 _____

2 _____

3 _____

4 _____

Now, if possible, ask your parents the same question, about yourself, and write down what they say: _____

_____

If possible, ask your grandparents the same question, and write what they tell you: _____

_____

_____

_____

_____

Ask the sibling you are the closest to, if you have siblings, and write what he/she says: _____

_____

_____

_____

_____

Ask your best friend, and write what he/she says: _____

_____

_____

_____

_____

Now, after all this input, ask yourself again. Trust your gut, and write everything you think is your genius:_____

_____

_____

_____

_____

_____

As you progress in life, you'll add to this. But this is a good start. Take a few minutes and discuss this final answer with a parent/mentor. This one thing can improve their mentoring perhaps more than any other!

Once this is done, stop reading for a day and take a break. This will allow you to internally ponder all these ideas and make them more a part of you before moving on. Tomorrow proceed to the next section, which is incredibly exciting! It is all about being mentored at a whole new level. But let's wait until tomorrow . . . .

A New Day: Mentored by Mission

A second key type of mentor is *mission*. Next to parent and spiritual mentors, this is the most important mentor. Having a feel for what your purpose is in life is so motivating, so exciting, so orienting; it becomes a great source of mentoring.

You were born to make a real difference in the world, probably in one of the following ways—or something similar to these below.

Read through the whole list once, and underline all that you feel are part of your life purpose.

- Feed the Hungry
- Clothe the Naked
- Empower the Poor
- Educate the Ignorant
- Promote Freedom

- ☞ Heal the Sick
- ☞ Comfort the Lonely
- ☞ Liberate the Captive
- ☞ Preach the Truth
- ☞ Produce Wealth
- ☞ Heal Families
- ☞ Increase Beauty
- ☞ Other_____

Now consider all those you underlined and circle the *one item* that you think most clearly describes your purpose in life. We know that it can be really hard to narrow this down; make a note of the ones competing for first in your mind and heart. Then narrow it down to one and circle it!

Of course, you'll probably do more than one of these in life, so that's why you underlined several. But the key to the exercise is to circle one—the one that most represents your "true north" for this time in your life.

By the way, it is okay if you change this focus later in life. But for now, your mission category helps you see right into your core!

Once you are done, and one item is circled, do the following: Ask your mother what her life focus is and what she feels yours is:

Mother's:_____

_____

_____

_____

_____

Yours (according to Mom):_____

_____

_____

_____

_____

Ask your father what his life focus is, and what he thinks yours is:

Father's_____

_____

_____

_____

Yours (according to Dad):_____

_____

_____

_____

Now, go back and circle a second item, so you have a total of two top areas of life focus.

These are two of your greatest mentors! They are real, powerful guides in your life.

Finally, if possible, meet with a parent and discuss all this with them. Be open. It is okay to change your mind, or to choose three instead of two, or whatever feels right to you. The only set guidelines on this are to really give it your time and attention and to discuss it with your parents.

Once you are done, put this away for today and give this time to assimilate and become part of you.

Do the next section in this chapter tomorrow!

ANOTHER DAY: MENTORED BY GRANDPARENTS

Another key type of mentor is the Grandparent. If you are lucky enough to have grandparents who are still living and involved, use their mentoring where possible. Unfortunately, in our modern world there is too often a huge gap between grandparents and grandchildren. This is sad because they usually have so much to teach you. The following will greatly improve your learning:

Ask your mother the most important lessons she learned from her dad. Write them: _____

_____

_____

Same, from her mother: _____

_____

_____

Your dad, about his mother: _____

_____

_____

Your dad, about his dad: _____

_____

_____

_____

Discuss with your parents how you can learn more from your grandparents, if possible: _____

_____

_____

THE FORMAL MENTOR

One more vital kind of mentor is your formal education mentor. This may be a parent or, if you're a teen, someone who meets your parent's approval. Here is what you need from your formal education mentor:

A Coach. Someone to meet with you one on one, listen to your questions and concerns, and help you make plans and follow through. We recommend that you meet with your mentor as a coach about once a week.

A Facilitator. Someone to help you have group discussions on readings at least 1-2 times a month and who reads the book (or portions of it) and participates in discussions.

A Leader. Someone to talk to about your dreams, goals, genius, purpose in life, personality styles, and everything you think about as you are growing, learning and figuring out your life.

A Manager. Someone who gives oversight to your schedule to make sure you aren't overextending and that you are studying hard, and to say "yes" or "no" to your proposed plans.

An Advocate. Someone who deeply cares about you, believes in you and will help you become your best. Someone who sees greatness in you, even more than you do, and will go to bat for you, find opportunities for you and help you become all you can.

A Guide. Someone who does 1-5 without pushing too much, manipulating or taking over your studies or life. Someone who shows the way and helps you ask the right questions and make your own good choices.

These are the things you should ask of your formal education mentor. Often you will have more than one person who fulfills a particular role on this list. Ideally, the Formal Mentor will fulfill all of them.

Take the time right now or very soon to sit with your mentor and discuss these six roles with him/her. Find out how he/she sees each role, and share your thoughts too. When you know you and your parents agree that you have the right mentor, follow your mentor's lead.

If you aren't sure who your mentor is, look for one. If you are a teen, have the discussion with a parent or guardian and ask them about it.

One of our favorite stories on mentoring is the old movie *The Karate Kid*. If you haven't seen it, rent it and watch it. Pay special attention to the trust that is required in mentoring, and to the concept of "wax on, wax off."

Other movies that teach about mentoring include *Dead Poet's Society, Hobart Shakespeareans, Finding Forrester, Stand and Deliver, Star Wars* (all), *The Karate Kid* (new) and even *School of Rock*. There are many others, as this theme appears to be one of Hollywood's favorites. If applicable, get your parent's permission to watch these, and where possible watch them with your parents/mentors and discuss what they teach about learning.

Great mentoring changes your life. If you want a truly great education, find and follow good mentors.

Great Mentors lead to Great Education; mediocre mentoring leads to mediocre education. For this generation, only great education is good enough. Don't settle for anything less! If you do, you will lessen your ability to fully become your best you.

4
FALLING IN LOVE

Jordan* didn't fit in with any of the popular groups at school, and even after his parents decided to homeschool him he struggled in the youth activities at church and in home school groups. Nobody seemed to like him, he thought. He just didn't seem to know how to fit in.

He begged his mom not to send him to "another stupid youth conference," but she made him travel all the way to the camp and attend.

Once again, the camp counselors were his only friends; the other kids met and broke off into groups of new friends while Jordan found himself alone at activities and meals.

At the talent show on the second night, Jordan wandered in late. He stood at the back looking for a chair, but they were all taken. Kids were laughing, and everyone cheered loudly as each talent finished. He wished he had signed up for a talent—he was pretty good on the piano. But it was too late now.

Jordan got tired of standing and walked up the aisle looking for a seat. The girl singing finished and the cheers stopped right when he reached the front row. There had been no empty chairs so he turned around to walk back.

> "I find as I grow older, that I love those most whom I loved first . . . . Reverence and cherish your parents; love your neighbor as yourself; and your country more than life."
>
> *Thomas Jefferson*

---

* Significant identifying details in this story have been changed.

That's when he realized he was standing in the middle at the front of everyone! The girl had returned to the audience, and the counselor hadn't yet stood up to announce the next talent.

Everyone was looking at him. And there he stood. In the silence.

Jordan realized that this was a disaster. At least before he had been anonymous. Weird, but ignored. Now he was ... he had no idea, but he knew it was *bad*.

He suddenly became ultra-aware of his 3-day stubble and the backpack on his shoulder. Nobody else in the whole audience was carrying a backpack. He choose this moment to look directly into the eyes of the blonde girl he had been watching the whole conference. He couldn't help it. He had hoped she might ...

He realized suddenly that he was staring at her and quickly lowered his eyes.

All of this happened in the split second he stood there facing the crowd.

There was no way out.

His mind raced. He couldn't just walk back down the aisle and stand in the back. He couldn't walk straight back to his room and stay there—though he really wanted to. He couldn't perform—he wasn't even on the list and the counselor wouldn't know how to announce him.

So Jordan did the only thing he could think of, he turned to face the stage and sat down cross-legged on the floor.

He waited for the talent show to resume, but things remained quiet.

He prayed that the counselor would hurry up and announce the next performance, but still he heard nothing. In spite of himself, he glanced back at the audience.

Something was happening.

Shawn was walking up the aisle.

Shawn was the most popular kid at the conference, Jordan thought. All the girls hung around him constantly, and he never seemed to even notice. Jordan had envied Shawn's ease throwing the football and the way the blonde girl always seemed to watch Shawn. He wished his own t-shirt would hang on his shoulders the way Shawn's did, with the vein in his arm always popping out. Shawn seemed to be Jordan's opposite in every way—with Shawn having all the good things.

"What on earth is he doing?" Jordan wondered. He could see the same question on the faces of the whole audience. The counselor still hadn't announced the next talent; and besides, Shawn had already played the guitar and sung so he wasn't going up to perform.

Shawn walked all the way to the front, with every eye following him. He paused slightly right next to Jordan, then turned and sat down.

Cross-legged, Shawn leaned back on his arms and watched the stage.

After a few seconds, the counselor got up and announced the next performer. Shawn and Jordan sat there together throughout the show. They cheered together—surprising Jordan. But it was fun, so he went with it. And when he cheered, Shawn looked over at him and smiled as they both held their arms high in the air.

Later, when Shawn motioned for him stand, Jordan nodded and they both cheered loudly together. Then they sat down for the next act.

Something changed in Jordan that night. It wasn't that the cheering was so fun, or that the girls asked him to dance later that evening; neither was it the way he heard himself talking at the book discussions the next day. Jordan wasn't sure what it was. Shawn never said anything or acted like anything had happened, even when they talked at meals or played volleyball together.

Jordan told his mom he was different somehow, during their long drive home. He told her, "They liked me," and "Claire gave me her email address!" He begged her to let him go again next year.

It is unlikely Jordan ever saw the tears of joy his mother shed. We know Shawn didn't.

So much depends on love.

A man who has run many youth conferences over the years shared this story with us. We were so touched by it. So much depends on love, on the little things love brings. Shawn didn't know Jordan before the conference, so it wasn't love of a specific person. But it was love.

Love matters.

So much—maybe everything—depends on love.

LOVE IS ALL THERE IS

This may sound crazy, but the secret to success is to fall in love, and then stay in love! This is really true. Have you ever felt how it feels to be really, deeply, head-over-heels in love with something? It is amazing!

That feeling often doesn't last a long time when you are young, but while you are feeling it there is nothing better. And honestly, at some point you want it to last for the rest of your life.

Now, this is the great secret of getting your best education! Fall madly in love with learning—and stay in love.

In contrast, here are seven ways guaranteed to make you hate learning:

1. Read everything from textbooks.
2. Get lectured to a lot, without any personalized attention or individualized studies.
3. Only study that which is required of you.
4. Plan the content in all your studies, and finish your plan as quickly as possible by doing the bare minimum.
5. Make sure you conform to somebody else's directions in all of your studies.
6. Do everything the complex way, the conveyor-belt way.
7. Study what others, especially those in authority, want you to— never what interests you most.

Sounds pretty terrible, doesn't it? We think it would be pretty hard to fall in love with learning using these guidelines. It would be like falling in love with a person using the following rules:

- ☛ Only fall in love with someone you are told to love by the authorities.

- ☛ Forget attraction. It's all about how the two of you score on some test created by experts. Trust the test!

- ☛ If you feel something special for someone, quickly squash any such feelings. That's all a distraction from what's really important—the expert's plan for your love life.

- ☛ You must love who you're told to love, because let's face it, the experts will choose so much better than you.

Sounds bad, doesn't it? But that's what sometimes passes for "good" advice on education.

Not here! Not in TJEd! Leadership Education is about passion and about following your interests. It's about falling in love with learning and *staying* in love with learning. It's about finding your true missions in life, the things you were truly born to do. Leadership Education is about using your passion to discipline yourself and really do the hard work and the hard things to become the real, genuine, best you.

One of the great Seven Keys is "Inspire, not Require"; that is what love is all about.

Leadership Education also uses logic, reason and good analytical thinking along with deep caring and passion in order to truly improve the world. Leadership Education is all about not settling for mediocre education, but rather having a truly great romance with great learning.

World-class knowledge, skills, understanding and eventually wisdom are the results of a truly great education. Of course, these things take a whole lot of hard work, tough practice and challenging study to obtain. They also come with a lot of fun—and they are truly worth it.

It is hard to get a truly great education—the kind you really want to have—when you feel like this:

"I'm just not good enough."
"I don't think I'll ever measure up."
"I wish I liked me more."
"I just don't see how to fit in with_____."
"If I had _____'s hair, or talents, then I could_____."
"If my parents would only_____, then I could _____."
"Why can't I be more like _____?"
"I'm just not good at _____."
"I wish _____."

It is so common and maybe even normal to feel things like this, but here is a secret: These deep and sometimes overwhelming feelings almost always go away when you fall in love! And yes, it works just as well to fall in love with learning as with a person. (In fact, a love affair with learning is, in most ways, a lot less complicated.)

There's room in your life, at the right time, for both; fortunately, you don't have to choose one or the other. When you want to feel really great, fall in love with a topic of learning or a favorite author, and just watch how the happiness flows.

The security in yourself, and the confidence in who you are deep down seem to just rise and constantly increase when you are in love with learning. And when you feel this way your studies, your family relationships, your social life and everything else just feel so much better.

When you are in love with learning, you feel happy; and when you are happy you tend to do the things that naturally bring more positives and happiness into your life and the lives of those around you.

Falling deeply in love with learning is for everyone!

Some may say that all of this is too idealistic, but chances are they are just scared of being hurt or somehow failing. It is true that many people have fallen in love, felt all these things, and then lost it all. Not wanting to be hurt any more, they talk and act as if it is all just an idealistic fantasy. But it isn't.

We are still so in love with our wives that it makes our teens sick! And we love our kids more and more as each year passes. Maybe you know parents who are that way too.

Well, learning can be just like that! It really can. We are both more in love with learning than when we were young, and we fall more in love with it every year. While we're not saying that loving learning is as important as loving your parents or spouse or children, we *are* saying that being in love with learning makes you feel great, incredible, confident, able, strong, and super excited about life and its opportunities!

HOW DO YOU FALL IN LOVE?

It has been said, "We love those whom we serve." This obviously applies in relationships with people; you can also apply it to your studies. If you want to love a subject, invest yourself in it. If you ever want to really succeed at something, whatever it is, you had better fall truly, deeply in love with it by giving yourself to it.

Success just takes too much commitment and hard work to do it without being helped by some incredibly strong force. Hate and anger can do it, but look at the horror and unhappiness they unleash on the world in examples like Hitler or Saddam Hussein. A drive for power or fame can do it, but again these will leave you and others so unhappy and the world a less pleasant place.

Love, on the other hand, is more powerful than any other emotion and brings *more* happiness to you and others. Take a look at the examples of Buddha, Christ, Aung San Suu Kyi, Paul Revere, Patch Adams, Mother Teresa, Robert E. Lee, Hariett Tubman, Gandhi, Esther, Madame Curie, Annie Sullivan and Joan of Arc, to name a few.

You can say that they did what they did because they had a love for it—and we believe that it's true. But we can attest that even in the best of "relationships"—whether with a person, a subject of learning or a cause—there are times when the sacrifices seem great and the rewards are either a memory from the past or a hope for the future. But selfless service to the right person, subject or cause brings about a sense of purpose and intrinsic reward that transcends the infatuation or immediate gratification that most people today believe are the hallmarks of a love affair.

WHEN DO YOU GIVE YOUR HEART?

It is so important at a young age to choose your allegiance. In fact, your allegiance is the most powerful thing in your whole life because it is the driving force behind virtually all of your actions, choices and even thoughts. If you choose your allegiance well and then stick to it you will be a great success in life. It is that powerful.

For example, the main allegiances human beings have are these:

1. Good/God/Love (whichever you prefer to call it)
2. Having/Self/Ego
3. Impressing/Others/Insecurity
4. Bad/Hate/Anger

It seems obvious, doesn't it, that only the first two make any sense at all, and that really only the first is a good choice? Well, it may be obvious, but still most people in the world don't choose number one. That's amazing. Even more shocking is that most people don't choose either one *or* two!

How can that be? How can it be that the large majority of people in the history of the world and around the globe today have had #3 (impressing/others/insecurity) as their primary allegiance and the central focus of their life?

The answer is really very profound: Most people don't consciously choose their allegiance. Let's repeat that, to let it sink in: *Most people don't purposely choose their allegiance.* They are born into and grow up in a society that teaches them that the most important thing in the world is the opinion of others and how well they fit in with others—and they just get used to acting as if they believe that.

We believe that the majority of people live their whole lives trying to fit in—with peers, friends, in school, at work, in career, at church, in their community and in nearly everything they do. They choose what to wear, eat, how to do their hair, how to talk, what to say and so many other things all based on trying to fit in or impress someone so they can look good to others.

Eventually, many people give away virtually their entire lives to be what they think others want them to be. Most aren't even aware that they are doing this, and as a result it can be said that they are not really sure of who they truly are!

What a tragedy. God, or the Universe or whatever you feel comfortable calling the powers higher than yourself, sees great needs in the world and sends a baby or sometimes a whole generation of babies to fix things. Then the babies get here, look around, and decide not to be themselves but rather try to be popular with and dependent on each other. Wow! What a mess.

The world isn't fixed, most of these babies grow up into unhappy adults, and little progress occurs—just because almost everyone just wants to fit in!

THE LOVE ALLEGIANCE

But it doesn't have to be that way. A few people have shown us a different way; they chose the Good/God/Love allegiance. Of course, just saying it doesn't make it so. A lot of bad things have been done in the name of Good, God or Love, but it is always done by people who are actually following another allegiance.

Specifically, the true followers of love give their lives to doing good and helping others be happy. They lead. They change the world. They do all this because they chose the right allegiance and gave their lives to it.

In the process, they become their real, true selves—the real them.

Leadership Education is all about finding and becoming the genuine you, the true you, *the Real You*. And the world will be changed for good if you choose the right allegiance and let the real, genuine you out!

WHY WOULDN'T YOU?

Why don't most people do this? We know this is deep, but we promised you we wouldn't sugarcoat things and that we would tell you the real deal. The truth is that most people are *scared*. They are deeply and persistently controlled by fear. They want so much to fit in, to get ahead. They are also afraid that they'll lose face or lose the material comforts they have.

These two big fears—of losing face and of losing things—keep too many people in dread and unhappiness their whole life. Why are there so many wars? So much pain and poverty?

Most people start out just wanting to feel accepted, just wanting to fit in, and then they build their lives, their careers, whole economies and nations around the fear of losing face or things. They aren't sure who they really are, but they do know one thing: They will fight hard to avoid losing status or possessions.

SELF-SERVING, OTHER-SERVING, HATE-SERVING

A few of these fearful people decide to do something to end their fear, so they choose allegiance #2: Self. They decide to ignore what others think, to reject fitting in and to make so much money or gain so much power that "nobody can ever take away their status or possessions."

Some fail in this quest, and return to the norm—spending their life energy to fit in with what they think will impress others. Some succeed, but find that they can never have enough money or power to avoid loss, or the fear of it. This life includes losses. Flat-out. Period. But even though they eventually learn this lesson, they still do much harm to themselves and others in their quest to serve Self.

Of course, the worst results come from those whose fears lead them to choose a life promoting hate, anger and evil. Very few individuals, maybe none, start out here; but as people lose in life and their fear of loss increases, some who originally sought just to fit in or to increase their own gratification or even just to feel more loved end up choosing to turn toward anger and hate. Usually they also expand their own pain and fear to others.

Fear is the great enemy. Fear leads people to remain stuck in the allegiance of fitting in, or to choose the allegiance of self. If fear continues, both of these motives can eventually lead to supporting evil.

For example, consider the German prison guards in Hitler's regime. Many followed at first because they wanted to fit in, later to keep their families from harm or to further their careers. Yet arguably all who followed did so out of the fear of getting into trouble. They did terrible things—inhuman things—that supported evil. "Hitler's" atrocities could not have happened without them. Yet it is doubtful that many of them started out hoping to be evil.

Fear leads to weakness and eventually can lead to evil. Only the strong choose good when life is truly hard and look to God/the Universe for inspiration to make that choice.

When Being a "Hero" Was Unpopular

Think of George Washington putting his name on the line against Britain. We tend to think of him as the popular leader of America, as its first president and the father of his country. But when he stepped forward to lead the revolution he was unknown in Britain, and later grew in infamy as the rabble-rousing head of a mob of wild-eyed hick revolutionaries.

Consider the unknown frontier boy Abe Lincoln when he first started, or the peasant Joan from a backward farm in France. What about the poor, unremarkable Agnes (later "Mother Teresa"), who was disliked by many of her fellow nuns?

The people in these examples chose Good, and the power of love coupled with ongoing inspiration kept them going. Without it they would not have succeeded as they did. It took great strength and courage to go against the norm, to realize that they weren't fitting in or impressing those in charge. They were vulnerable—facing powerful opposition—and they were openly criticized, disliked and persecuted. But they did it anyway because their allegiance was to love.

They were each truly *themselves*. This is what Leadership Education is. Gandhi, Jesus, Lincoln, Joan of Arc, and many others even died to bring love to this world.

Of course, most who choose the Love Allegiance aren't famous and don't suffer like this. Most are regular men and women, or boys and girls, who choose to follow good in the world and end up spreading goodness in family, business, career, community, media, education, church or perhaps even just by walking down the aisle to rescue a boy at a youth conference.

The following story was told to us by the director of a series of youth conferences—a totally different narrator and venue from the Jordan story, but familiar in the spirit of love.

Marie* was a foster child, and her caseworker called to make sure she was given the best counselor possible. She'd been badly abused as a child, and still carried the scars all over her body. Her face was so disfigured that "kids always avoid her or pick on her," the official said.

"Our kids are different," I promised before I hung up. I hoped it was true. I prayed long and hard about the counselor, even though I usually left these assignments to the camp director. Finally I decided to do just that—leave it to the inspiration of the camp director.

The one thing I did to intervene was to pull aside Marie's assigned counselor the first day of the youth conference and tell her, "Pay attention to Marie. You'll have a real story to tell if you do." She looked at me funny and said, "I pay attention to all my girls. They're all a great story." I smiled, happily rebuked, and knew it would all turn out great.

I watched.

---

* Significant identifying details of this story have been changed.

Meals were fine—the girls seemed to be including Marie. She seemed to enjoy the speakers, nodding and even smiling occasionally. But I still worried.

At the last meeting, where the kids had the chance to share their thoughts and feelings spontaneously and openly, I was surprised when Marie stood to talk. Immediately two friends stood up with her, just like they had done with the other girls that day. It just caught on when one girl cried and her friends went up and supported both arms.

Anyway, Marie stood and began to talk. I don't remember it word-for-word, but here is what I recall.

Marie said, "When I first came here I hoped someone would like me. Then I got my hopes up when a lot of you smiled at me the first day. I'm used to almost everyone turning away and avoiding me. It's obvious why," she said, pointing to her face as she said this.

"Then, the night of the dance, everything changed. You see, I have come to realize that my counselor is God."

I was used to youth saying some extreme things, but this was quite a statement! Her camp counselor looked as shocked as the rest of us when she said this. I waited to see what she meant.

"The night of the dance I tried to hide in my room. People had smiled, and been nice, but I knew no boys would dance with me. With so many pretty girls here, I didn't blame them. Why would they?"

She was crying at this point, and so were a lot of people.

"Well, my counselor Sherri came and found me and tried to get me to go. She said everyone else had gone to the dance, and that when she didn't see me there she came to find me. I made excuses but she wouldn't leave. She just kept telling me to come.

"Finally, I pointed to my face and asked if anybody would want to dance with *this*. Then Sherri did something amazing. She looked right at me, cocked her head to one side and got a real analytical look on her face, as if she was considering how I looked. I'd seen girls look at each other that way a lot, but nobody had ever looked at me like that.

"Then she said, 'I see what you mean; your hair *is* kind of lame.

I have some product that might fix it. Let's go to my room and see what we can do.'

"When she said that, something inside me just melted." Marie was sobbing now, slowly telling her story between sobs.

"I've had adults try to be nice to me before, and it was kind of them, but it always felt a little fake. But with Sherri, well I think she really meant it. I mean . . . really. So I went with her and she re-did her hair with the gel while I did mine the same way. Then she said it was beautiful and we headed for the dance.

"I was still scared, so I stopped walking and told her I didn't want to go. She tried to talk me into it, but I said no. She said she had an idea for my makeup, and I could see she wasn't going to give up.

"Finally I said to her, 'Sherri, thank you for all of this. It means the world to me. Really. But we both know it isn't my hair or makeup or clothes or anything like that. Sherri, I'm ugly. We both know it. The abuse made my face ugly. I know it isn't my fault, and I know I'm a nice person inside. I've been told these things forever. But my face is still ugly. It just is, and no boys will dance with me. If they do, it will be because I'm the dance charity case. So please, can I go back to my room?'

"Well, Sherri just looked at me, then she asked, 'Marie, do you believe in God?'

"The question was so unexpected, I just didn't know what to say, or why she would ask it. So I just said, 'I don't know, do you?'

"'Yes I do,' Sherri said, 'and I believe God wants you to go to this dance. I promise you that boys will dance with you and want to get to know you.'

"I just stared at her. She held my eyes and wouldn't look away. I could tell she was convinced.

"Somehow her confidence convinced me too. Boys would dance with me and actually want to get to know me. I couldn't imagine how it could be true, but Sherri's confidence made me want to at least go and see.

"To tell the truth, I wanted it to be true so bad that I just convinced myself it might happen. 'Okay,' I said, and we walked the rest of the way to the dance. I just kept telling myself that it could happen, over and over in my mind.

"When we got there, it looked fun. The music and lights were exciting, and many people were dancing and laughing. Sherri led me to a group of girls and we began talking with them.

"Then someone tapped my shoulder and I turned to see one of the boy counselors. He asked me to dance. I was so excited I turned to smile at Sherri, but she wasn't there. Later I noticed she was going from boy counselor to boy counselor and having long talks with them—then they would look over at me dancing, but by then I didn't even care.

"The first boy was so cute, and he danced three dances with me before the next counselor cut in. Each of them asked me questions, and answered mine, and I could tell that regardless of Sherri telling them to dance with me they really did want to get to know me.

"Then some non-counselor boys asked me to dance. Sherri swore to me later that she told the counselors to ask me but not the other boys. The way they acted when I asked them about it, I believe her. Anyway, it doesn't really matter, because they really cared about me and wanted to get to know me. They really did.

"They might not have been attracted to my face, but they were attracted to the real me and wanted to be friends. I never felt like a charity case, not in those conversations we had. Those were real. Thank you! Thank you all so much!

"I felt so loved at this conference . . . thank you." She paused and sobbed.

Finally she spoke again. "So if there is a God, Sherri — I hope he is a lot like you." Then she sat down.

I don't think any of us who experienced her sharing that day will ever be the same.

THE GREATEST POWER

Love is the greatest power in the world. Falling in love with learning will make your education and life great! Anything else will be mediocre in comparison.

Falling in love with your life, with the Real You, and living to be who you were really born to be is what life and a great education are all about.

There is a quote that just about sums up the power of inspiration. We don't remember who said it, but the idea was that if you want to build a ship, don't focus on plans or workmen schedules or where to get materials. These things are important and need some attention, but your focus should be on helping your whole team fall in love with the joy of being out on the deep sea!

If you fail at that, the rest of the details will be difficult to manage, but if you succeed at that one thing, all the rest will fall together effectively and with a fraction of the effort. Inspiration and love are just that powerful.

THE TEACHER LEARNS

Oliver learned this truth while teaching writing classes. At first he had used a more conveyor-belt model and taught one of the most boring courses he'd ever mentored on grammar, punctuation and sentence diagramming.

Later, quite by accident, he noticed something really interesting. A student in his history class told him he wanted to write a paper on a science topic that deeply fascinated him. For some reason Oliver gave his consent. When the paper was turned in, it was excellent in content, organization, style, punctuation and grammar.

Oliver asked the student about the quality (as his writing had been far from excellent in the past), and he said that he had learned these things in the writing class. When Oliver expressed skepticism, the student finally clarified, "Well, maybe I didn't learn it from *the class*; but I wanted this paper to be really good so I just looked in the books from the writing class and all the technical rules were right there."

The next time Oliver taught a writing class, he did it very

differently. He assigned the same books on style, punctuation and grammar rules, but he never used them in class or in his assignments. They never even diagrammed a sentence in class. Instead, on the first day of class he asked the students: "Who is really excited to write about something that really interests you?"

He had those who did write about their topic of interest. When they were a week into the course, he held up the grammar books in class and mentioned that the more the students cared about their topic and paper the more they should apply the rules in the books.

That's all he ever actually did with those books, but the students used them a lot. He would sit around a large table with the participants in the class and read, on a volunteer basis, the latest works of the students, inviting discussions on how to improve the voice, tone, organization, technical precision, etc. Nearly every paper turned in reflected the rules with relatively few errors. He found that if he pointed out the errors once or twice, students (whether they were the authors or the commentators when the improvements were discussed) almost never made them again.

This really works. Details are vital, but they fall into place more quickly and effectively when we love the overall project! Inspiration works. As Thomas Jefferson put it, *"Nothing is troublesome that we do willingly."*

On the first day of class, Oliver always had a few students who said they really weren't interested or excited about writing anything. At first, he gave them assignments or tried to get them excited, but it didn't work.

WHAT DO YOU LOVE?

He then learned to do something that always had amazing results. After telling those who where were excited to go ahead and write, he would ask the others in the class to share what they *were* excited about. Whatever the answer, he told them to pursue it. They still participated in the table discussions, but he told them not to write until they had something they really wanted to write about. Until then they were to read, research, and do whatever they felt excited about.

Almost every student he ever did this with eventually got really passionate about writing something and did. The students' writing drastically improved in the process.

It is amazing how much better we do at something if we are inspired because we *love* it. Maybe this isn't really all that surprising after all. Nobody likes to be forced or made to do things they dislike, right? Why should education be any different?

Choosing to Love

Even when we need to study things that don't excite us at first, if we have learned the skill of falling in love with the things we should, then the sky is the limit! This is cliché, but it is also true.

Great teachers and mentors are great because they care enough to inspire you; then you do the hard work of great learning because you love it. We doubt there is a more effective method. And you don't have to wait for great or inspiring teachers; you can seek them out!

Teacher or Topic?

After excitedly paying for a huge, weeklong seminar event, Oliver spent a great deal of time deciding exactly which classes he would attend. There were over a hundred to choose from, and he waited in long lines to get into the ones he wanted. By the end of the second day he was exhausted and frustrated. His friend, who was attending with him but had a different class schedule, was still excited and loving the event.

"Why are you enjoying this so much more than I am?" he asked.

"Oh, that's easy," the friend said. "I never choose a class by topic. I learned a long time ago that a great teacher makes even the dullest topic really fun for me, so I always choose classes according to the teacher."

Oliver followed that advice for the rest of the conference and loved it! It made waiting in lines totally worth it. He has used this method ever since, and it works. Sometimes, of course, the important thing is not how "fun'" the teacher is. Some of our best teachers were "boring" presenters but had such depth to their knowledge that it was incredibly inspiring to be in their class.

The key is inspiration. If a teacher, coach or author is inspiring to you, you'll have the best possible experience. If you know you need to read a certain book or be in a class that doesn't seem inspiring to you at first, find a way to get inspired about it!

If you go looking for inspiration on something important, you'll find it. It just works this way. Kind of like, "when the student is ready, the inspiration appears." It really is true, but sometimes you have to seek it.

If you don't find inspiration at first, keep looking. The word "inspire" means literally to be "in spirit," and when you seek something you eventually get into the spirit of it.

For example, the story is told (true or not) that when a student came to Socrates asking to be mentored, Socrates grabbed the young man and dragged him down to the beach and into the water. Socrates had been a rock cutter, and was very strong. He held the young man under the water until he passed out.

When the boy regained consciousness, he bewilderedly asked why Socrates would do such a thing. Socrates told the boy that when he wanted knowledge as much as he had wanted air he should return and ask again.

This is a dramatic (and currently illegal) way to make a point, but the point is worthy of consideration. Only when the student *really* wants to learn and is inspired to learn will the mentor be of greatest help.

FALLING IN LOVE, AGAIN

The key is to look for inspiration, not something else. This brings us back to falling in love. If you want to excel in math, find a way to fall in love with it. Often the way to engage a topic that seems, shall we say, outside of the scope of your natural interest, is to learn the human story behind the subject. Learn about the lives of the great scientists, mathematicians, the great artists, statesmen, war heroes, religious leaders, etc.

This is one reason that classic fiction is often the most read of the classics list—the stories speak to us. But what ever it is you feel called to study—if you want to really learn Shakespeare, or whatever—find a way to fall in love with it. Find a teacher who loves it; find a work that interests you for the human interest of it; find a way to invest yourself so that you can fall madly in love.

Shanon really wanted his kids to learn math and science well; but even more, he wanted them to *love* it. So what did he do? He hired the wackiest math and science teacher/mentor he could find. This guy did not call himself a teacher; he called himself a lover of math and science. Do you see how this works?

The man, David, didn't just *love* math and science; as Shanon's kids would later tell, he *breathed* the stuff! His day-to-day life was built around everything math and science. Did his love of math and science rub off? It was impossible for it not to. Did Shanon's kids learn math and science? Of course. Do they still remember David and the lessons he taught years later? With great fondness.

The key is not trying to figure out how to learn math, science or even Shakespeare, but rather trying to figure out how to fall in love with math, science or Shakespeare. That's where to put your energy. Later, once you are in love with the subject, you will naturally find ways to learn it better, to learn it *well*. But at first, fall in love with it. That's inspiring!

Truly falling in love with learning is central to getting a great education and having the life you were meant to live. We make a point of getting a great education because it is so incredibly important!

INSPIRE, NOT REQUIRE

Several years ago, Shanon was teaching the concept of *Inspire, not Require* in a seminar in Canada. A mother was very upset because her two boys seemed to not enjoy reading and spent most of their time skateboarding. She was afraid that if she didn't force them to read and study that they would never choose to do so on their own. Shanon was trying to make the point that inspiring is often a case of "match, latch and lead," validating the boys' love for skateboarding and then slowly inspiring them to expand their horizons. She was adamant that he was wrong and that it would never work.

Six months later, when he returned for a second seminar, the same woman was there and offered a public apology. It turned out that she decided to try Inspire, not Require and began showing sincere interest in what her boys were doing. Not long afterward, her sons began filming their boarding ventures, which eventually led to an entrepreneurial marketing business that required a real education to operate. They became inspired, and then took action that led to quality education and application to their life's work.

The world needs what you have to offer, and your education will determine to a large extent how much you can give the world. Your leadership is needed; that involves the Real You—not just a dumbed-down version of you that wears masks and is trying to fit in!

There are so many ways to be the Real You, to find your true you and live a life of love and make a great difference in the world. Of course, it all starts by doing the hard work to get a great education. And even that is a lot of fun if you are in love with learning.

THE INNER RING

But the goal of fitting in is a real temptation. In fact, it may be stronger among teenagers than any other group. We're sure you understand all this because you are probably living it.

C.S. Lewis once wrote a challenging essay entitled "The Inner Ring." He cautioned that the danger of trying to fit in and be what others want us to be is that there is no end to trying to fit in. As soon as we figure out how to be a part of group A (by conforming to their rules), we will suddenly see that group B (or even group A1) is even *cooler* and then find ourselves chasing the carrot on the stick all over again.

This can lead to a life of never being satisfied and seeing ourselves as failures. On the other hand, Lewis teaches that being our true selves is fulfilling, calming and productive. Lewis called the people who truly know who they are and what they were born to do "sound craftsmen."

Because this challenge is so strong for teenagers, it is the perfect and best time to understand it and win the battle. Right now is the time to clarify your true allegiance, decide to choose the right one, and make that choice work. Now is the time to be the Real You, not try to impress others or hide behind masks.

WHERE WILL YOU BE?

There will be other Jordans and Maries in your life, others who stand alone in need of friendship or help. And where will you be? Sitting in the audience watching? Wishing somebody would help? Pointing your finger and laughing, maybe? Perhaps you will say that you aren't as popular as Shawn, that you couldn't make such a difference. Or some other fear will hold you in your seat.

But let's be clear with each other. We all know where we should be, don't we? Walking up that aisle to sit with that boy . . . even though we don't know him. Even if others point and laugh. Even if . . . well, no matter what.

It's doubtful any of us will ever see that exact situation again, but there will be many like it in your lifetime! Many opportunities will rise for you to act, to serve, to make a difference. Your generation was born for this, as were you *personally*. We don't know what the situation will look like. We bet someone will be in need, and it will take courage for you to act, and your fears will tempt you to hold back. We bet you won't listen to the fears, however. We bet you will stand and do the right thing. We believe your courage is up to the task. But more importantly, we believe your love will lead you to take action when such needs arise.

When your life's path crosses that of a person or situation where you could lead and help and serve, we bet you'll stand and walk up that aisle. That's what your education is all about. We hope you get the kind of education that will lead you to stand and walk forward, not even realizing that you are literally saving somebody's life.

We hope we see you someday at the front of the crowd, sitting cross-legged, next to Jordan . . . .

5
SCHOLAR PHASE

You may have read Oliver's book *A Thomas Jefferson Education* or the book *Leadership Education* that he wrote with his wife Rachel. If so, you are familiar with the Phases of Learning and the levels of Scholar Phase. While these books were written mainly for your parents, teachers and mentors, in this chapter we will focus on the Phases specifically as they apply to young people who are right now (or soon will be) in Scholar Phase. We think you will really enjoy this.

The first Phase we call Core Phase, which is all about learning right and wrong, good and bad, true and false, and how to tell the difference. The next Phase is Love of Learning, where you learn to fall in love with learning. We covered this in the last chapter. The next two Phases are Scholar Phase, which we will cover here, and Depth Phase or college-level mentored studies.

All the Phases are very important. Of them all, Scholar Phase is the least worked on and the most needed in modern times.

> "Be assiduous in learning, take much exercise for your health, and practice much virtue. Health, learning and virtue, will insure your happiness; they will give you a quiet conscience, private esteem, and public honor. Beyond these, we want nothing but physical necessities, and they are easily obtained."
>
> *Thomas Jefferson*

Who's a Scholar?

Let's start by clarifying that when we speak here of Scholars, we mean people in Scholar Phase—not professional academics who make their living researching, studying and writing about a certain specialized field of expertise. We have great admiration for such scholars, but that is not what we mean by Scholar Phase.

Leadership Education covers the different kinds of college/ university mentors, including scholars (the deep experts in certain fields), coaches (who focus on personal support of individual students), teachers (who emphasize classroom teaching), and philosophers (who live for new ideas, models, patterns and connections).

Ideally, mentors have a little of all four of these, and a primary focus and particular gift in one of these areas. We think these and other styles of mentoring have some real merit; we also think that students gain most over the long term by working with more than one or two types.

When we speak of Scholar Phase, we're intending the more philosophical meaning of the word used in the phrase "a gentleman and a scholar" and in the martial arts tradition of left hand (scholar) covering right fist (warrior). Our greatest martial arts instructor often quizzed us on why the scholar is more important than the warrior, and he used the U.S. President as a civilian commander-in-chief as an example. His answer was that strength must always be led by wisdom.

The reason we chose the term "Scholar" Phase is that in our modern world where many people talk of leadership, few promote the great education which leaders need to not only gain followers but to lead them in the right direction! Scholar Phase is all about starting to become a person who can truly lead people well and rightly.

The Task of a Lifetime

Mastering this skill of leading is a lifetime task, and the purpose of Scholar Phase isn't to complete your learning, but to so immerse yourself in the habits of great learning that you keep using them to solve problems, improve yourself and your conditions in life, and to help others do the same for the rest of your life! That's Scholar Phase.

Shakespeare wrote, "Be not afraid of greatness: some are born great, some achieve greatness and some have greatness thrust upon them." Taking a page from that book, Howard Gardner has taught about the different ways people become leaders, including:

1. those who just feel like they were born to be leaders and spend their whole life preparing,

2. those who are surprised when leadership roles come to them, and

3. those who don't want to be leaders but find that they are needed.

As you may imagine, all three types do so much better in leadership if they have the benefit of a great Scholar Phase.

And make no mistake; you *will* be called on to lead—whether you want to or not. The world needs leadership, and you were born to be a leader in your unique way. Preparing with a Scholar Phase is hugely important.

5,000 Hours

Quantitatively, we believe Scholar Phase takes about 5,000 hours of studying. That is not a "complete" education—perhaps nothing ever is. But it is more than most people get and it is a good start. In comparison, a high school student who studies (intensive, personal, sit-down study) for two hours a day, five days a week, nine months of the year (180 days) will have studied 360 hours a year—or 1440 hours at the completion of four years of high school. Many high schools are only three years and we haven't diminished the count for the inevitable holiday breaks, but we're giving them the benefit of the doubt.

That, including personal reading, is actually higher than the national average. Still, it is only just 29% of a Scholar Phase.

Of course, if you count time sitting in class as study, the number goes up. But we count very little of class time as deep, personal study. The purpose of class time in great education is not study, but rather 1) inspiration, 2) answering questions, and 3) more inspiration.

The conveyor-belt model of education does it exactly the opposite of Leadership Education: it uses 5-7 hours of class time a day to inspire 1-2 hours of personal study. Even if you have great mentors who know how to use class time for colloquia* and simulations, Socratic questioning or small-group interactive projects—like some private schools and a few visionary charter schools use—that still only adds up to about 3,000 hours of study in four years.

Students who put a lot of effort into debate, theater, forensics, music or other substantive, skill- and attribute-building extracurricular activities also get additional Scholar hours.

But truthfully, almost nobody really does a true Scholar Phase anymore. That is why community colleges and universities in our generation spend the first two years on increasingly remedial "general ed" courses—they need students to have the basic, foundational knowledge before they can progress. Unfortunately, most students don't get a full Scholar Phase even with four years of high school *combined* with two years of college.

Indeed, most students only finish a true Scholar Phase (5,000 hours of deep, personal study and a deep level of basic knowledge) somewhere in the senior year of college. (If you're older, now is a great time to start!)

THE LOST DEPTH PHASE

This is a real tragedy. It means that most American college graduates have a poor to mediocre Scholar Phase and a college major, but no Depth Phase. (Interestingly, international students who attend American universities are often way ahead of Americans in math and science but have less background in the humanities; they also seldom

---

colloquia (singular: *colloquium*): small and medium size group discussions about something all the students have read or experienced

get a Depth Phase at American universities, but rather a "Finite" or "exclusive" Phase in their major.)

Depth Phase is vital if you want to train a nation of leaders, but not so important if you want an upper class that controls government, big business and the lower classes.

American colleges and universities are acclaimed by many as the best in the world; but the truth is that their emphasis for most students is primarily remedial general education and "Finite" Phase majors and graduate training.

The difference between Depth Phase and Finite Phase is very important. Finite Phase focuses on one topic in depth, training experts in one field—from accounting to law to dentistry to botany, etc. This is vital for an advanced, specialized and technologically-based economy.

Depth Phase does exactly the same thing, training experts deeply in one specialty; but it does so with students who have already been through a Scholar Phase education—who already possess the broad understanding of human history, ideas, philosophy, the arts, the scientific and numerical fields, biography and ethics, leadership and economics, governance and technology, etc.

HISTORICAL PRECEDENT

The difference in results is drastic. As Allan Bloom pointed out in his classic bestseller, *The Closing of the American Mind,* the last society to be as highly trained (Finite major studies) and as poorly educated (no Depth Phase) as the current U.S. was Germany in the 1930s. A significant number of German engineers were highly enough trained to build cutting-edge weaponry, submarines, missiles, airplanes and so on, but not well-read enough in history to vote against Hitler or refuse to do his bidding.

Same with German scientists, who understood chemicals and genetics enough to experiment on their neighbors when they were thrown immorally into prison camps, but not learned enough in ethics, morals, history, psychology or basic politics to not elect Hitler or refuse to torture their countrymen.

Critics could say that by the time submarines were being launched and people were being tortured, it was too late to do anything. But only the combination of top technical training and poor Leadership Education could have allowed this all to happen. A less highly-trained people *could* not have done it, and a truly educated people *would* not have done it.

This may seem extreme to some, but seriously, what is education all about? If it is not to teach us what is good, ideal, and right, then it isn't really education. People with a real Leadership Education would say "no" to such a state of things. Period. Anything less is poor education.

UNABLE TO STAND

Another painful example of this is the Hungarian Revolution of 1956. While the citizens were able to repel the communists for a time, it was their lack of general Leadership Education that not only allowed the communist invasion ten years earlier, but also ultimately prevented the Hungarians from keeping their oppressors at bay. Courage and bravery and heroism were all plentiful, but solid leadership had been replaced with ignorance, suspicion, mistrust or lack of common bond. It was one more example of the destruction of a civilization in modern times.

Without widespread Leadership Education, the regular people and the highly-trained experts end up following the dictates of those in power.

Just study any society that provided its youth a Leadership Education, and compare it to those that didn't. For example, look at the American Revolution (with many Americans having received a Leadership Education) versus the French Revolution (where the revolutionaries were mostly uneducated).

They Got It Right

Or look at the great example of the thousands of Japanese-American citizens interned in relocation camps during World War II. Attacked by the Empire of Japan at Pearl Harbor and full of suspicion, the U.S. government relocated and interned nearly 120,000 Japanese-Americans under very difficult conditions. Most of them were American citizens. They were uprooted from their homes and businesses, unjustly confined and treated as enemies of the state.

However, because these families promoted Leadership Education in their homes, had a sense of community and followed their inner sanctity of life, they understood the causes of their situation and rather than fight back or cause trouble, these citizens banded together, improved their situation and ultimately sent 15,000 young men to fight in heavy combat in the battlefields of Italy.

These young Japanese-American soldiers proved to be among the most valiant of all the American forces during World War II, suffering an unprecedented casualty rate and receiving over 18,000 individual decorations. These families showed that even when the world was falling down around them and they were being mistreated, they could still have dignity, honor and do the right thing.

To juxtapose the experience of the Japanese Americans with the privileged class in Hitler's Germany makes the comparison even more poignant, and the contrast obscene. The WWII-era German people considered themselves highly educated but were in fact just highly trained. They had highly-skilled learning, but no Scholar or Depth Phase. In fact, they didn't know that they didn't know.

Education For A Future Of Our Choosing

Education matters. And we would do well today to closely consider what type of future we want. Abraham Lincoln is credited with saying that to foresee the future of government one should watch what is being done presently in the schools. Though we can't find an original source for this quote and it may not even have been Lincoln's original thought, there is a lot of truth to it! Today's schools are training but not educating, which is the path of Hitler's Germany.

The solution is to educate and train. Both are good, and they naturally support each other. We need our youth to have a Scholar Phase, then a Depth Phase, and then specific training for their career by choosing a major and then graduate school. Together these support freedom and prosperity.

In fact, this was the model in the founding generation of America. It all hinges on Scholar Phase in youth, which allows Depth Phase and career studies in the college years—just like Thomas Jefferson's education.

FREE ENTERPRISE V. FREE EDUCATION

This changed in about 1854, and since then two great views have battled for control of America: free enterprise versus free education.

Now, whenever someone says that something is free, it is wise to read the fine print. Free often means that *you* don't have to pay for something, not that *nobody* paid for it. So when something is free, find out who paid for it. Sometimes free just means that you don't have to pay for it right now—the bill will come later. This is usually the case on anything offered by the government, like free education. You don't have to pay tuition to attend, but you'll pay taxes for schools for the rest of your life. Of course, this isn't necessarily or always bad; it's just important to be clear.

So, what kind of freedom were these two competing views offering America? Well, free enterprise follows the New England model Tocqueville and Jefferson prized so much. In his great classic *Democracy in America*, Tocqueville said that New England was the model for the future of America and freedom around the world. In free enterprise, you are free to enterprise things, to take initiative and act. As long as your enterprise doesn't hurt someone, you can do it.

If you want to make more money you can enterprise something

to do it, like start a business, seek a job, change careers, gain a skill, invest in somebody else's enterprise, move to another place, boldly go where no one has gone before or whatever you want to enterprise—as long as you don't hurt somebody.

That's freedom the free enterprise way. It includes the freedom to succeed, and the freedom to fail and start over. No matter what your race, gender, lack or abundance of money, family background or social ties, you are free to take whatever enterprise you want as long as it doesn't take away the inalienable rights of another. The founding generation called this "the pursuit of happiness."

Unfortunately, the second view has spread widely. "Free education for all" was first widely promoted in modern times by Karl Marx. He taught that it could be used to give all children the same education, thereby getting rid of the rich and poor classes. He promoted government oversight and running of such schools, to control the curriculum and ensure equal education to all.

He also said the government should require all children to attend these schools, so there would be no rich private schools or poor non-schooled. He promoted society of a single class controlled by the government (knowing full well that the government itself was an aristocratic upper class controlled by a party).

THE SOVIET CONVEYOR BELT

This plan was carried out in communist nations, but ironically it was also adopted by many free nations with one change: Elite private schools remained, along with the new free government schools. All children were required to attend one or the other, and since private schools were costly, only the wealthy used them.

Under this system, two types of education flourished. Elite schools prepared future aristocrats using broad Leadership Education combined with upper-class values, while free schools trained the masses to get jobs working for the upper class—either directly or indirectly.

The American Class System

In the United States, leading proponents of the class system (which the founders had successfully reduced in power) saw this as a way to resurrect aristocratic power, and they have supported its growth and expansion.

Some may disagree with this and say that America doesn't have aristocratic tendencies. But consider where such naysayers want their children to go to school. If their eyes are set on prestige, what could be more aristocratic?

America was once considered free because the president of the country had the same educational background as the average American. Today there are two education systems—mass job training for followers and elite education for the upper classes. The mass education doesn't facilitate Scholar Phase or Depth Phase, but instead provides generally shallow basic education with finite job training. Actually, many employers would agree that the job training isn't really all that deep, either!

The Third Option

There is also a growing third option, in the diverse forms of non-traditional models of education like:

- home schools
- the growing number of non-elite private schools
- some charter schools
- commonwealth schools
- entrepreneurial learning on the job
- non-accredited schools and colleges (one of the fastest growing sectors of the U.S. economy at the time of publication)
- coaching and mentoring services, and
- many new online educational opportunities.

The twenty-first century has been called an information age and sometimes a digital age, but so far it has been mostly an age of crisis. Our national consciousness was poised in anticipation of crisis and looked for its advent in the Y2K scare. In reality it did not materialize until 9/11, but since that world-changing day we have seen a tide of tremors and aftershocks ever since. What we need is a Wisdom Age, a season where many or even most of the people have a Scholar and a Depth Phase. The wisdom that would result would change everything!

LET'S TALK ABOUT YOU

Let's get specific about *your* education. If you are in a public school and you want to get a Leadership Education, you need two things:

1 a good mentor to help coordinate all your studies and activities, and

2 to do a full 5,000-hour Scholar Phase.

If you are in private or home school, or just reading as an adult, you need these same two things!

Then, when you are done with Scholar Phase, you should seek a college program or equivalent reading where you can do a true Depth Phase—5,000 more hours combining the greats in all fields, with a mentored, college level of study, and deep expertise in the field of your major or planned career. Graduate school can bring even more expert training after that.

There is a drastic difference between the skilled expert and the truly wise expert! The difference is a great Scholar Phase before college and a great Depth Phase in college *before* career training. Those who get this will be much better prepared to lead than those who only do basic general ed courses and a major. The future of freedom and prosperity are truly at stake.

Anything less than Scholar and Depth Phase is mediocre, and you were born to be great—not mediocre.

Where To Start

So how do you get a great Scholar Phase? Well, start with the Teen 100 Book List in Chapter Two. Just start. That's Step 1.

Step 2 is to find a mentor. This is someone who can help you plan your weeks, days, months and years to get a great education. Parents are often the best mentors for Scholar Phase. Even if you get a mentor who isn't one of your parents, your parents are still the best ones to help you choose such a mentor.

Whoever your mentor is, recommend to them that they read the following:

- *A Thomas Jefferson Education*
- *Leadership Education: The Phases of Learning*
- *The Student Whisperer*

Structure Time

Step 3 is to structure time. Plan a set amount of time to study each day. We don't recommend planning specifically what you are going to study each day very far in advance; that can really ruin the excitement and feeling of inspiration. Instead, consider having just one place where you keep all your study materials and books—a shelf, a desk, a cabinet, an old box, whatever. We favor a bookshelf, since you can see all the titles at once.

If you can, put the shelf or box or whatever next to the place you'll be sitting to study. Then each day when it is time to study, look at the shelf and go to work on something from it. Add items to your shelf whenever you want. As you get tired of a book during your study time, put it back on the shelf for now and pull out something else to study. Put notebooks or file folders with writing or other projects on the same shelf and use them the same way.

From time to time, take stock of your frequent choices and how you feel about the emerging patterns. Does your emphasis feel like a sign of a mission direction? Does your tendency to pass over a particular subject feel appropriate for the season, or rather like you should seek to be more inspired to engage it?

Every day at the allotted time come to your shelf, get things to study, and then study. If you are going to a library or away for a few days, pull several items off the shelf and take them with you in a backpack. Don't miss your study time!

BY THE CLOCK

How much should you study? Start with what you can. If you aren't able to do more than two hours in a sitting, you might want to review the Phases and make sure you're well established with your Core and Love of Learning Phases. If you are thirteen and new to Scholar Phase, we suggest starting with about 4 to 5 hours a day of sit-down study. Then build up over time. Our seventeen-year-olds have typically done 8 to 10 hours a day, 4-6 days a week, eleven months of the year. But you need to personalize what works for you. Adult readers: Schedule whatever you can. Work with your mentor on this.

A good Scholar Phase in four years could be done in six hours a day while age 14, five days a week for nine months with a long summer break. Then at age 15, seven hours a day, five days a week for nine months. Age 16, eight hours a day, five days a week for nine months (which by the way is the same 1440 hours in just one year of study that a student would get during 4 years of studying 2 hours a day after school). By this time you've studied over 3,700 hours since age 14, and you have a year left.

For age 17, you can do nine hours a day, five days a week, but we would suggest instead, 10 hours a day for four days a week supplemented by some longer, full-day or two-day activities on things that really interest you. Either way you'll get over 40 hours a week and over 1400 hours this year.

Fill In The Gaps

Finally, at age 17 or 18 we recommend that you cut your daily readings back five hours and spend 3-5 hours a day on areas of weakness to "fill in the gaps." And adult readers may take longer but can still do this by reading some each day. Everyone has gaps. Everyone!

Consider this: If you mastered absolutely everything in a regular public school 12-year program and remembered every detail, there would still be a whole world of learning that you know *nothing* about. Even if you spent your whole life learning and innovating on what you learned, you would never master All There Is To Know. You would still have gaps. No matter how or what or where you learn in your childhood, you will arrive at the brink of adulthood with gaps in your education. And by this time, you will probably have a sense of which of those gaps are most significant in your preparation, and how to prioritize your learning in Transition to Depth Phase.

For teens, here is a little hint that could help you: At the beginning of this year, we suggest you take several sample ACT or SAT tests, and study for them during half your study time this year. Or, if you score really high on all topics at first, you may want to apply directly to college. In fact, you might do all of this during age 17 and go to college when you are 18.

Follow your own pace, and don't push faster than you enjoy! Of course, as an older youth with a solid Love of Learning, some of the "enjoyment" might be grueling, but that's your call. Again, the key is to plan the time you will study and follow through. If you need to adjust time, don't hesitate to do so.

For example, at seventeen Oliver's daughter Emma was studying math for four hours a day as part of her college prep. Over time it seemed to him that she was sort of losing the sparkle in her eye and the spring in her step. Oliver would ask her how her studies went each day and her smile would disappear and her shoulders would just slump. He could tell something was off.

They talked about it a lot, trying to find the problem. Her math studies were becoming drudgery, but she wanted to accomplish some lofty goals that year and she was highly motivated to do it. She had really enjoyed math previously, but now was feeling overwhelmed.

Oliver suggested that she cut her time on math from four hours to three each day. She did, and her smile and enthusiasm came back. Of course, she was studying other things lots of the day; her overall hours in study didn't actually diminish, but that one-hour shift in emphasis made all the difference.

And guess what? Her math scores started improving much more quickly! She literally started learning *more* in less time.

LOVE OF LEARNING OR LOVE OF DAD?

Shanon learned from earlier experiences that some of his children were highly motivated to please Dad. He misread this and unwittingly contributed to a study overload. Fortunately, it was discovered early with no lasting damage done. Now he is very careful to ensure that the study programs his kids adopt are motivated by their Love of Learning, and not just their Love of Dad. Fifteen-year-old Ginnie, for example, is a voracious reader and when allowed to choose what she studies, reads an average of thirty books a month. This she characterizes as "having fun."

Of course, most students are not in any serious danger of studying too much, and we've also seen learning improve by adding more time! So pay attention, consult with your parents/mentors and adjust your time of study as you find what works best.

OUT OF THE BOX

Now we're going to ask you to think a little bit paradoxically. One of the 7 Keys is "Structure Time, Not Content." Having an elaborately-programmed schedule for your studies will likely break down your love of learning, squelch your creative leaps and inhibit your inclination to follow a line of study as far as your interest will take you. That being said, having a plan and a goal that informs your choices is not always a bad thing. For example, Oliver's oldest son, Oliver James, always structured his Scholar Phase with an hour of math first thing, followed by study of whatever he wanted from his plan for the rest of his scheduled time. In monthly mentor meetings Oliver and O.J. reviewed the subjects and content covered to look for meaningful patterns and consider if plans and goals should be revised.

Emma never "scheduled" this hour of math before Transition to Depth, though math studies were always part of her shelf.

When it came time to study for the ACT/SAT, young Oliver was ahead of Emma on math. She caught up after a few months, but it was hard work. So don't hesitate to add an hour or more at the beginning or end of your study time of a topic you want to emphasize. For adult learners, the fact that you may have less time to read than most teens is mitigated by the reality that you don't have to concern yourselves with grades, credits, or SAT exams. In addition, your life experience will greatly enhance your ability to understand and apply principles from what you read.

THINK

Step 4 is to start measuring and improving the quality of your thinking. There are three main ways to do this, and they really work. The first is to take lots of notes as you read, then run your ideas by your mentor. You will be amazed at how much this increases your thinking ability.

You should schedule set times to meet with your mentor to do this, like every Monday morning from 9-11 a.m. or every fourth Saturday from 1-5 p.m. One of your parents, or both, may be glad to do this, or they might help you find a special mentor for this purpose. This is so helpful—don't skip this great tool!

Second, set up and attend group colloquia on the books you

have read. Even if only three or four of you meet and discuss, this can be so very powerful. You will learn so much by hearing what other people learned from the same book you read. Do this for as many books as possible, sometimes with the same group of people on a regular basis and other times with new people. This is most powerful face-to-face, and also very good online with your peers. Include adult mentors and parents.

Third, write papers, or even just mini-articles or blogs on topics from the books you read, and send them to friends and your mentor. Ask for feedback, critique and rebuttal to what you have written. Again, you will be so amazed at how much you learn from this. Rewrite based on the feedback you receive, and keep rewriting until your work is of the highest quality.

Together these three actions will greatly increase the quality of your thinking, speaking, communication, analytical reading and writing. Thank your mentor for having you rewrite things to increase the quality, and ask her to do so if she doesn't already.

It isn't so much *how* you study, as it is how well you think and the quality of your writing (and other projects) that matters. Use these three tools to greatly increase the quality of your thinking.

YOU, NOT THEM

Step 5 is to take responsibility for your own education, and to take the initiative to go get the great education you want and need. Your education is up to you, not someone else. Remember the motto, "You, not Them." Don't wait for parents, teachers or others to *give* you a great education. Go get it yourself. Ask for help, listen to guidance, but don't wait around for others to get it done.

SIMPLE, NOT COMPLEX

Getting a great education is so simple! Read and study the greatest works from the greatest men and women in all fields—math, science, the arts, history, literature, scripture, everything. Really learn from the greats. Take notes as you study, and discuss these notes with your mentor. Write about things you learn, and share your writings with mentors and friends. Practice skills that require repetition, like math problems, memorizing the chemical elements, history dates, public speaking, drawing well, performing in a play or concert, writing business plans, etc. Attend colloquia and discuss, discuss, discuss. Put in enough time each day.

That's it. Simple.

Yes, this is hard work, but it isn't complex. It just takes follow through. And by falling in love with learning, you make all of this really fun!

Out of these simple things, a great education comes. And the impact of these small things is a great influence on the freedom, prosperity and happiness of many.

There is nothing our world needs more than young people who take initiative and get a great Scholar Phase—intellectually and morally! This one thing can change and improve the world drastically. It will change and improve *you* drastically, for sure. This one thing makes it possible for so many other great things to get done.

You are too good to settle for mediocrity, or anything less than a truly great education! It is all up to one key person: You!

6
FINDING THE REAL YOU

H
ave you heard of the great teen questions? They are all about helping you find the Real You. The true, genuine You. That's what the teenage years are all about. If you find that, *when* you find that, you'll be an adult. You'll be ready for your life's mission, or at least ready to get ready! When you find that wonderful and powerful person, the Real You, you'll be on the path to greatness.

This brings a whole new level of meaning to the principle of "You, not Them." Your life is not about all those other people and what they want you to be, all those masks you are tempted to wear. Some people wear masks for others their whole lives, never quite figuring out who they really are.

That's why the great teen questions are so important. Actually, "teen" or "teenager" is a relatively new name for these questions, because they've been around a long time. The term "teenager" was first used, as Dr. Gary Chapman reports, in 1941 in *Popular Science*

"Nature has written her moral laws on the head and heart of every rational and honest man, where every man may read them for himself. If ever you are about to say anything amiss, or to do anything wrong, consider beforehand you will feel something within you which will tell you it is wrong, and ... this faithful internal monitor ... will guide a man clear of all doubts and inconsistencies."

Thomas Jefferson

magazine. Before the great depression, youth were usually considered young adult children of their parents' family until they got married.

When the Great Depression took away most jobs, and nearly all the employment of those in the teen ages, this group became its own social demographic. It stopped focusing on work and turned more to play. This generation was first called the "bobby socks-ers," because girls this age wore short skirts with high socks and danced to big band music. Then its members were called "teensters," then "teeners," and finally "teenagers" in 1941.

THE BIRTH OF THE TEENAGER

Just to put this in historical context, the word "teenager" came out in January of 1941, and Pearl Harbor happened almost a year later in December of 1941. A good history of all this is found in the appendix of *The 5 Love Languages of Teenagers,* and also some in the *Oxford English Dictionary.* Another good commentary on "teenage" history can be found online at www.TJEdforTeens.com, in an article written by Dr. Michael Platt.

Anyway, the terms "teen" and "teenager" were created by advertisers to market to this separate group that was more interested in "games, music, milkshakes, wearing moccasins everywhere," and "driving like bats out of . . . ," as *Life* magazine reported in 1941.

When the modern economy created teenagers during the Depression, it also created something else: the midlife crisis. It all starts when a teenager decides to put on a mask, or several masks, usually in order to "fit in," and it often ends in a painful midlife crisis somewhere between 35-50 for women and 40-55 for men.

In the midlife crisis, the person, who stopped being his or her true self as a teen, reaches a point where s/he can't handle the pain of 25-40 years of hiding behind masks. The person just breaks. The projects and momentum that had consumed his/her energies for two decades are no longer sustainable, and they begin to falter—whether it be in the context of business, family roles or a grand identity crisis.

He is tired of struggling in a job that wasn't really what he wanted, or being at home with kids that she wasn't prepared for, or living a life that wasn't planned out but fallen into by a series of other previous unexamined choices, being pressured more and more by uncommitted to and unchosen demands of others and watching any hidden feelings or dreams slipping away.

MIDLIFE CRISIS

As he breaks, the person in midlife crisis often hurts everyone around him—leaving spouse, children and church and doing whatever he thinks might ease the pain. The stereotype of a person in midlife crisis is that of alienating family, driving a sports car too fast, listening to the music of the person's past teenage era and finding a love interest from a different age group. There is a reason that this looks a lot like being the wrong kind of teenager—it is because the person never answered the great teenage questions and is emotionally and developmentally stuck.

If you answer these questions before you are twenty years old, you can enjoy your adult life and avoid this struggle later. It is very sad when someone doesn't do this! And these questions are so worth answering, regardless of your age.

The person in midlife crisis goes looking everywhere for something—anything—to help her ease the pain. And do you know what helps? Answering the great teenage questions! It would have been so much better to have just learned them as a teen.

Not everyone finds these lessons or learns them as a teen or even later. Sadly, many men and women go on in this painful struggle for the rest of their lives. The truth is, we were each born to be somebody, someone important, someone wonderful, with a unique and vital life mission and purpose. And that someone for me is the Real Me, and for you that someone is the Real You, and until we find the real us, we will be unhappy.

If we try to be someone else, it just plain doesn't work. It hurts.

A lot. And we never seem to find happiness or real peace until we start being our true selves. Teenage "fitting in" doesn't work at any age! We need to be real!

FIT IN OR FIX IT

The great teen questions fix all that. We call them the teen questions because they are the great questions you should naturally work out and answer before the age of 19 or 20. If you do, you naturally find the Real You! And that makes all the difference. If you're older, answer them right away.

Unfortunately, this really is the road less traveled, especially in modern high school environments. Most people in our modern world live behind their masks for a long time, only finally answering the great teen questions after midlife or even later—or not at all.

Shanon has taught this very concept to many adult groups—the concept of people spending their teen and early adulthood years hiding behind masks, not knowing their true selves. In every case, the vast majority of the audience has completely agreed that this is happening to themselves and almost everyone they know. They also virtually demand to know what the questions are. They want to answer them for themselves!

In fact, there are adult questions to answer later, but these will stay stuck until you can answer the teen questions. You can read more about these questions and the basic issues of development in the writings of three great classic psychologists: Jung, Piaget and Erikson.

You may find that answering a few of these questions is easy, but answering all of them is challenging. Still, answering them all is exactly what is needed.

So let's get started.

We brainstormed several ways to do this, wrote some of them and then deleted them all and brainstormed again. We wanted to make sure this would work. Finally we decided to just tell you the questions and let you decide how to answer them. Just knowing the right question is ninety percent of the battle, and you are smart enough that giving you the questions is all you need from us. You can figure out the rest better than any set structure could.

These are the right questions. Few of them can be answered with "true/false" responses or numerical "right" answers like in math. Nor will essay answers or even well-worded verbal answers suffice. To truly answer the great teen questions, you have to really dig deep into yourself.

The thing is, you are already asking *yourself* these questions. Your real self, the Real You. Your mind, the thinking part, is doing the asking. And your mind needs to listen to what the deeper, true you has to say in response.

THE REAL YOU

These are pondering questions. Take the time to really ponder each before moving on to the next. Here's how:

- make a copy of the following pages with the great teen questions
- cut along the lines to get one question per strip of paper
- put all the strips in a small box or can
- for the next 22 days pull out one strip from the box and make it your question of the day
- you really need to take a day on each in order to truly listen to the Real You and answer the question, so don't rush this
- take more than one day if you ever feel that you need more time to really answer the question
- ask the Real You the question, and ponder and really listen for the answer
- during the day, write down all thoughts you have on the topic
- show your mentor the question of the day and listen to her thoughts on it

- spend the day really thinking about the question, and writing answers along with your other activities

- in the morning, look yourself in the eyes in a mirror and ask the Real You to please answer this vitally important question

- include the question in your prayers or meditation for the day

- each evening write down your answer

- each morning, read yesterday's answer before drawing today's question

- keep all of these answers in one notebook together, leaving blank pages between each question so you can add more later

- amend your answers as new thoughts and feelings come, even on later days when you have a new question of the day

- when you have completed all 22 of these great teen questions, read through the whole notebook of answers and make changes

- re-read the whole notebook each day for one full month, to get the answers deeply ingrained into your thoughts

- you will be drawing these in random order on purpose, as all 22 great teen questions are vital and each person who does this exercise will have his own unique and powerful experience

Do not skip this exercise. Even if you are a male, do not skip this! It will have a huge positive impact on your success and happiness.

Once you have set up your box with the great teen questions cut up and ready to draw, feel free to keep reading in this book. You may even finish the book before your 22 days are up, and probably before the month of reading your 22 answers each day is complete. That's okay. But don't skip this exercise—it is vital that you answer the great teen questions now in your youth!

Do I live with integrity, or do I fudge things when it seems like it might help me?	Do I generally trust or mistrust the universe and my future?
Do I use ingenuity to overcome problems, even big ones, or do I get frustrated and give up or just expect someone else to bail me out?	Do I use blame, or have I learned to focus on doing the right thing now and letting go of all blame, anger and stress?
Do I know my allegiance, absolutely and clearly?	Do I know that I have the power to create my best future, or do I spend my time doubting, worrying or feeling shame?
Do I take initiative and do whatever needs to be done or that I want to do, or am I constantly thinking about my inability or waiting for others to lead out?	Do I say mostly nice things about myself openly and inside my head, or do I think or say a lot of bad things?
Do I feel approved of by myself, or do I seek a lot of external approval from others or achievements?	Do I know that I am great and humbly accept that I will do great things, or do I fear being great or fear being mediocre or less than others?
Do I openly admit my mistakes, or do I try to hide them or justify them?	Do I spend my time looking out for and helping the "little guy," or do I participate with others in looking down on people or being cocky or thinking I'm better than others?
Do I know I have a great mission in life and that to do it I'll need a great education, and am I taking action to get a truly great education?	Do I complain or whine, or do I let go of frustrating things and focus on doing good?

Do I judge others, or do I look for ways to love and accept them?	Do I do things just to impress others, or do I make decisions based on what I want to do and what I think is right for me?
Do I allow myself to get bored, or do I take charge of my time and stay happily engaged in doing good?	Do I learn from my mistakes, or do I keep making the same mistakes over and over?
Do I win well, or do I gloat, act cocky or arrogant, or think I am superior to others?	Do I lose well, or do I get angry or sad, or choose some other negative reaction?
Do I take smart risks, or do I avoid failure at all costs?	Do I worry about what others think of me, or do I make choices based on what I think is right—regardless of what others may think?

Feel free to read the rest of this chapter and book while you are still answering the great teen questions. But don't skip this exercise! If you are doing that, stop here. Do not pass Go; do not collect $200. Go directly to jail. You are staying in the rat race. Go back to the great teen questions and do the exercise! You'll never get out of jail or the rat race without it! (If you've never played *Monopoly* or *Cashflow*, try them!)

In the real game of life, only the Real You can truly succeed or be happy. Do not cheat yourself by skipping the great teen questions.

NUMBER TWENTY-THREE

There are many personality tests, and some of them really good. Most of them are fun. You may have taken the Briggs-Myers test, or the color code, or discovered from a personality test that you are a "parrot" and your mom is a "golden retriever" and your brother is a "rabbit." You may have studied the famous Sufi personality model called the Enneagram. (We really like this one.)

You may even have studied the four Greek types, or the tribal types of earth, wind, fire and water. We really enjoy Mary Beth Jones' work using this model. You may even have studied personality typing more deeply in a psychology book, or attended a lecture or seminar on this topic.

Maybe you've taken an IQ test and been grouped by it, or read books on cycles like *The Fourth Turning* and learned that you're from the warrior generation and mom is an X'er or a Boomer. Or maybe you haven't read about personalities before and this is your first introduction to them.

Whatever your background in personality studies, we want to suggest that all of these and many other personality tests and books are a valuable way to learn about yourself—as long as you enjoy them, learn from them, and don't take them altogether *too* seriously.

Now we are going to answer great teen question number 23*: What is the true personality of your "Real You?"

Just because you test as an "introvert" or a "red" doesn't mean anything in your life is set in stone, that you have to always be what the test says, or that you follow that pattern in every situation or role in your life. Personality can be fun, enjoyable, and teach you a lot about the Real You, but always remember that you are you and John is John and María José is really María José. Types teach us, but each person is really himself or herself—not some type.

This applies to the types in this chapter as well! Don't ever let types add to your masks. You are the real, genuine you; and while studying psychology or love languages or personality types can inform your self-analysis and your approach to relationships, no test will ever completely define you—or others.

---

* We should note that we are using the Hebrew numbering system on this. It has 22 total characters, each with its own unique meaning. In some traditions it also has a special 23rd character, seldom used but meant to encompass all the meanings of the other 22! When you study Hebrew, which we hope you will someday, you can learn more about this.

We think one of the best things you can learn from personality books and tests is how many types there are, and then use this to grow and develop character traits that you want to develop. If a test tells you that you are a "yellow" or an "otter," it is still a lot of fun to go practice and develop the "blue" or "lion" talents. The Real You can always grow and improve! In fact, we're sure the Real You wants to.

Here we want to introduce one of our favorite personality models. It's one we've compiled from our study of various religious and tribal traditions. It is a little different than any we've seen elsewhere, and we think you'll enjoy it and learn a lot about your Real You from it.

We're going to just list different types, and we want you read through the whole list and underline any that might be you.

Ready? Start underlining:

- leader
- administrator
- operator
- wisdom
- faith
- healing
- miracles
- technology
- art
- prediction
- vision
- languages
- service
- government
- writing
- speaking
- teaching

- warrior
- comforting
- prince/princess
- orphan
- messenger

How many did you underline? That's great. It is fun to see all of the areas that you might excel in. Now go back and circle the one that you think is the most you. **Remember, only circle one—the one that you think is the most you.**

Was it hard to circle just one? Was this fun? What does this tell you about yourself?

Now, go back and circle one more, for a total of two. What does this tell you about the Real You?

Finally, go back and circle one more, so you have a total of three circled: write them below:

_____ – _____ – _____

This is your type! Again, what does this tell you about the Real You? Together these are called archetypes, meaning great models or examples like Adam or Eve archetypes, or Achilles or Caesar or Penelope archetypes. For a longer list of archetypes pulling from the Greek tradition, see the writings of Caroline Myss.

Look again at the top three archetypes you circled. Together these form your type. Did you circle all these as the Real You? Or from a mask of you? If a mask, go back and do the whole exercise as the Real You! The Real You type is:

_____ – _____ – _____

Finally, one more thing. Who are your greatest heroes? (The heroes of the Real You!) Write them below:

1 _____

2 _____

3 _____

4 _____

5 _____

6 _____

What do each of these heroes teach you about the Real You?

Who is the Real You? This takes years to fully understand, of course, but answering the great teen questions gets you where you should be now. After you have completed these exercises, be sure to share them with your parents or mentors. Perhaps you may feel to keep some of it to yourself for a time; but share some of it. You will learn a lot from your parents' thoughts on this, and they will be better mentors because they will understand you better.

Be sure to answer all 23 great teen questions by completing all the exercises in this chapter. It will greatly improve your life and future leadership.

The best you is the Real You, and you have great things to accomplish in this world. The world needs you. Never worry that you won't measure up; just focus on becoming the Real You. As you do, everything else will fall into place.

As you answer the great teen questions and become more and more the Real You, you will be truly amazed and thrilled at who You really are. At the same time, you will be amazed and thrilled at who others really are too! By being more authentically in tune with yourself, you will have an increased ability to see, and help bring out, the greatness in others. Together with them, once you've answered the great teen questions for yourself, you will have much more power to truly improve the world.

7

SUCCESS IN THE NEXT TWENTY YEARS

H istory runs in cycles, and there is a pattern of four seasons repeated over and over, each about 20 to 25 years long. Like the seasons of the year, one naturally follows another and each feels different, and accomplishes a different purpose in the grand scheme of things. In their book *The Fourth Turning,*[*] authors Strauss and Howe call these four seasons "turnings," like turnings on a cycle. We strongly recommend you purchase and read this important book. The four seasons are:

1st: Founding. New institutions are built up to solve the great problems that culminated in the last crisis, like the United Nations, Social Security, World Bank, International Monetary Fund (IMF), NATO and other organizations created right after the Great Depression and World War II. Lots of businesses flourished in this period also.

"To no events which can concern the future welfare of my country, can I ever become an indifferent spectator; her prosperity will be my joy, her calamities my affliction . . . . Nothing makes me more happy, than to render any service in my power, of whatever description."

Thomas Jefferson

* ISBN #978-0767900461

2nd: Awakening. Youth grow up and challenge the old establishments, like the counter-culture movement of the 1960s at Woodstock, or the Civil Rights movement iconically led by Rosa Parks and Martin Luther King, Jr. among others, and strong pushes for Feminism and Environmentalism, etc.

3rd: Unraveling. Two big viewpoints and political parties fight for power, and everything seems like it is coming apart. Economies boom. The last unraveling happened between 1984 and 2001, and the one before that in the "Roaring 1920s."

4th: Crisis. Big problems come. Actually, crisis seasons usually consist of three crises in a row, sometimes overlapped. First is the wake-up crisis that shocks everyone, like the Boston Tea Party, the election of Abraham Lincoln or the 1929 stock market crash, which started the Great Depression. In recent times, it appears that 9/11 was likely such an event.

Second comes a major economic crisis, and then third, usually a major war, pandemic or a mixture of these and other calamitous elements all at the same time. The last several crisis seasons include The Revolutionary War and subsequent Depression, The Civil War and Depression, and the Great Depression and World War II. Sounds bad, huh?

GOOD NEWS, BAD NEWS

We live today in a crisis era, and if you are now a teen you will grow up and start your life, family and career in a Crisis or Founding season. The good news is that a Crisis Season has always been followed by another Founding, just like winter is always followed by spring!

The bad news, which is also the biggest challenge in all of this, is that when the Crisis comes, almost everyone over thirty years of age is totally immersed in the rules, conventions and patterns for success of the *last* phase. This means that even though the economic boom times and long periods of peace are apparently over for a time, most people keep making choices that reflect what *used* to work—even though now all the rules have changed.

They make a lot of ineffective choices, because they don't *realize* that the rules have changed. For example, parents educated in 2nd or 3rd seasons often think that their kids should see education as job training. For 4th and 1st seasons, however, that is a big mistake. In these seasons, teens need to be prepared for entrepreneurship and initiative much more than job-specific skills. There are many other differences between seasons.

Here are the leading rules of success in each turning. In each season, success is found in:

2nd and 3rd: Big Institutions, Professional Careers, Investment, Credentials and Resume, Leisure and Entertainment.

4th and 1st: Family and Community Relationships, Entrepreneurial Ability, Initiative and Leadership Skills.

The way to fail in 4th and 1st seasons is to try to live in the rules of the previous seasons. The way to succeed is to engage the new reality. As teens, you may need to encourage your parents and grandparents with this!

Those who will thrive in times of recession, depression, slow-growth economies, even war and other major crises are the ones who focus on home, community and entrepreneurship.

Again, the problem is that older generations define success the old way: A good major in college, good career, fun entertainment almost every evening, a really nice house, several new cars and good retirement. They also want the same for their kids. This is a 3rd Season view. It will be generally available again, if the cycles hold true (as they have for over 3,000 years) somewhere around the years 2070-2080.

The generation before them saw success as public schools that were central to the community, a stable job at one company for life, husbands supporting families with wives staying home and savings in the bank and home ownership as the best investments. This is a 2nd Season view, and it will come back again somewhere around the years 2045-2055.

As for real life from now through the 2020s, 2030s, 2040s and maybe into the 2050s, it is time to get real! Success now, and for most of your life, will be determined according to the rules of 4th and 1st Seasons. The new 4th Turning society and economy is here, and the new realities with it. These new realities need all your idealism and enthusiasm, but they can't and won't be like the past, which too many adults are desperately trying to cling to, or just beginning to mourn over. Those days are gone.

THE LONG VIEW

Another key of leadership is to focus on what's next, not on the past or even the challenges of now. Overcoming current challenges is important, but the focus should be on what's ahead. As with the examples of Henry Ford and William Gates, who rode the swelling tide of a season that they anticipated with an energetic vision, those who thrive from now to 2029 will be the ones who focus on and embrace the rules of the coming 1st Season ahead!

Be one of those who thrives, and help others do the same!

Because of the cycles and seasons, some of the more important classics to study as a teen are those written during 4th and 1st Seasons or by authors who lived through them.

One of the best of these, with a focus on family and entrepreneurship, is *Our Home* by C.E. Sargent.

Sargent lived through the 4th Turning of the Civil War period and built his career and family in the 1st Turning which followed. His book is one of the Great 100 Teen Books listed in chapter two.

Following are fourteen "rules" for financial success, family leadership and overall happiness in 4th and 1st seasons as taught by C.E. Sargent. We have added a lot of commentary to these, geared specifically for our time. Still, all fourteen of these guidelines apply to any 4th and 1st Turning period in history. These are so much more helpful than many of the things suggested today for success by 2nd and 3rd season experts.

Embrace The New, The Now

First, embrace the new. Then, embrace the now. Forget 3rd season goals. They are gone, over, done, and it is time to move on. As a teen, you may not have gotten caught up in a lot of 3rd season planning, but if you did it is time to embrace something else.

Those who pine away for the old will not succeed, nor will those who wait around for the old days to come back. Forget the old measures and methods of success, and get excited about the new opportunities!

Second, spend evenings and Sundays with family. This principle is so simple, and yet so powerful. People bond naturally in the evening, and in our modern world the best entertainment is family time.

So much in financial and career success in 4th and 1st seasons depends on family support and relationships, and close bonding is vital. Such bonds also build a closer community around the family, and this is also needed for financial and social success in this season.

For example, in the small community where Shanon lives, families are very close-knit. It is common to see them taking walks as family groups nearly every evening. The community does a lot of things together: baseball, community festivals and parades, local fund-raisers and neighborhood parties, etc. Tough times are easier for them because they know how to work together, and there is a communal wealth that is greater than the sum of what each family separately has. Shanon remembers that when he first moved there it snowed about three feet in two days. Before city employees could begin the process of removing snow, family members and neighbors had already dug out the sidewalks and driveways of the widows and the elderly.

Third, strengthen your self-culture. In 2nd and 3rd seasons, much of life is built around popular culture, fitting in, looking "right" to others. In contrast, in our time true happiness is much more important than impressing anyone. Figure out what makes you happy, and live it!

Fourth, clearly articulate and write out your individual rules for life. Plan them. Live them. Leaders are needed, not conformists. Your family, community and those around you need you to know who you are, what you stand for, and for you to truly stand for something. Of course, true leadership and excellent rules include conformity to core morals and goodness. Decide what is most important to you, who you really are, and be it!

RAISING ADULTS

Fifth, instead of raising children, the focus of families will be on raising adults! Children in this view are under 12 years of age. After that the goal is helping young people become adults. This means that the teen years won't be seen as times of all fun and games, but rather, teens will be considered young adults who are needed to help the family succeed, and who actually contribute to the society in general in meaningful ways.

In addition to their education, they will help the family flourish by doing a lot more work than the last three generations of teens. Also, the educational focus will be less on training accountants, attorneys or engineers and more on preparing youth to become good parents and wise citizens. Indeed, in 4th and 1st seasons we need 18 year olds who can go to war, lead communities, start businesses, etc.

Some might see this as a loss of youth, but that is just old seasons' thinking. In truth, teens flourish in 4th and 1st seasons because they are given opportunities for leadership and responsibility—what every difficult "teenager" of the past forty years has been protesting he is ready for!

Sixth, make Meaning a central focus of your learning, conversations and thinking. In 2nd and 3rd seasons the emphasis is often on prosperity and "getting ahead." In crisis times the national emphasis shifts to things that really matter.

Tests, trials and struggles provide important lessons and the opportunity to consider what is truly important and what isn't.

Look for meaning in everything, and you'll often find it. Learn to be grateful, to see the "silver lining" in challenges, to learn from mistakes, to get up whenever you fall down and just keep trying.

The 4th and 1st seasons are great times to turn to great classics and learn the best lessons of the past.

REACH OUT

Seventh, spend a lot of time serving widows, orphans, grandparents, the elderly, the sick, and any who are down or struggling. These should be the focus of much family time and personal discretionary time.

In 2nd and 3rd seasons these are simply service projects, but in 4th and 1st seasons they create true community—much more than an after-work project once in a while. Make this one thing a priority in the 4th and 1st seasons, and you will find happiness and thrive in other ways too.

Boredom is a 2nd and 3rd seasons' disease. Bored? Go serve. Make service the default. If you have nothing else to do, serve. By the way, doing something that seemingly blesses only you *is* doing something worthwhile. But if you are just looking for entertainment all the time, start looking for things to do that help other people. Sometimes the best service (and most entertaining activity) is spontaneous service.

If there aren't enough projects already organized by others, organize some yourself or with a group of friends. Or, just pick a small, unspectacular task—such as visiting an elderly person and engaging them in conversation to help ease their loneliness and keep their mind sharp. Don't wait on this one—get started right away.

Eighth, make marriage the central focus of your life. Even as a teen, preparing to be a great wife or husband is a vital project. Note that the focus usually changes with the seasons:

2nd: Job over Parenthood
3rd: Parenting over Spouse

4th: Spouse

1st: Ideal Family Roles

In 4th and 1st seasons families grow stronger, and a large part of this is that spouses really need each other and turn to each other for help. This blesses all levels of family. Unfortunately, a shift to such times often starts with a lot of marriage struggles—unless people understand and apply these fourteen principles and other guidelines of good relationships.

The key is to maintain the primacy of this relationship even after marriage. This doesn't decrease the value of parenting, but in fact increases it. Truly bonded and united spouses do the best parenting.

IMPACT

Ninth, get a true Leadership Education, what you might call an Impact Education. Consider the varying focus of education in different seasons:

2nd: Job Training

3rd: Career Training

4th: Family and Community Forms

1st: Societal Forms

Both Impact and Leadership Education include the skills of initiative plus ingenuity, tenacity, quality, creativity, persuasiveness, etc. Nothing teaches this as effectively as classics, mentors, simulations and the Seven Keys covered in earlier chapters. Indeed, Leadership Education was specifically designed to prepare people for success in challenging times.

Tenth, engage entrepreneurship. This is a must for almost everyone in 4th and 1st seasons. Even those with stable jobs, which are much fewer in these seasons, seldom find that their stability equals true prosperity or fulfillment, in the sense of building something together with spouse and family that contributes value to society. In the Fourth Turning and beyond for several decades, a majority of people will have to be entrepreneurs or intrapreneurs to maintain a standard of living that was considered normal and desirable in the past several decades. And the family unity and individual growth will pay dividends for generations to come.

Note that different generations have very different views about entrepreneurial ventures. Here is what being an entrepreneur means to most people in the different seasons:

2nd: "You can't get a real job!"

3rd: "Build a business and sell it, retire young."

4th: "Entrepreneur to survive, until the economy is better."

1st: "Build a business to change the world."

The key is to adopt the 1st season view, no matter when you are entrepreneuring. It is the one that really works. In a 4th or 1st season, it is vital to adopt this mindset for your career, whatever it is—even if you have a stable job (only employees with this view will keep the company stable). These types of employees are called "intrapreneurs."

In 4th and 1st seasons, entrepreneurship is the key to survival and also success. It requires all the skills and knowledge that naturally come from a good Leadership Education. The best place to start as a teen is the great reading list in chapter two of this book!

BE A PRODUCER

Eleventh, produce wealth. Seriously, there is no time to create and build wealth like 4th and 1st seasons (this is easiest in 3rd seasons, but much of the wealth created then is lost as quickly as it is gained; besides, the next 3rd season will likely come in about the year 2070).

It may seem strange to emphasize producing wealth in times of recession, depression, war and challenge, but that is exactly the best time. This is not to say that you should put greed first, but rather that in such times a focus on entrepreneurial building is exactly what your family, the community, the society and the nation need most!

In 4th and 1st seasons, building businesses is among the most charitable and patriotic things you can do for society. People desperately need jobs and nations desperately need successful businesses.

More than anything, the world needs the Leadership Education that you can only gain by building something! The classics are a great start, but once you leave the sanctuary of Scholar Phase youth, some of the best Leadership Education is found in building organizations and making them work!

This is called being a producer, not just a consumer, employee, dependant or victim. Author Dennis R. Deaton calls this having an "Ownership Spirit." He writes in his book by that title:

> *"When we think in Owner terms, we live independent of circumstances. The ups and downs of the day don't define who we are, our mood, demeanor, or commitment. When something goes awry, Owners can be disappointed and frustrated, but they don't find someone to blame or resent, as Victims often do. Owners tend to focus their thinking on what to do—what options they have and what courses of action to pursue.... When people treat them rudely, Owners seldom take offense. They could, of course, but they see that as a waste of time and energy.... Owners understand that life is not easy, and they don't expect it to be."*

In addition to this vital mindset, society needs wealthy philanthropists more than ever in 4th and 1st seasons, and people who are creating value and wealth. Society needs you to be a producer or an owner.

Of course, the popularity for creating wealth is different in each of the seasons:

2nd: Savings and security for the family (from a steady job and bank savings accounts)

3rd: Money to retire young and relax (from entrepreneurship and/or investing)

4th: To help the needy, by giving them jobs and where needed, charity (by building and growing a successful business)

1st: To build society, including the needed new institutions of strength after the crisis season (by building and growing businesses)

Twelfth, develop your creativity and inventiveness. This is needed so much in 4th and 1st seasons! Creativity is needed to find ways to be more frugal, individually and as a society, and also in producing things, money, jobs, wealth, philanthropy, etc.

Creativity and inventiveness are needed in finding ways to give yourself and others their needs, wants and luxuries. They are necessary to fix society's problems and to take advantage of its opportunities.

A Season Of Opportunity

Times of challenge are always the seasons of greatest opportunity, and success at such opportunities depends on your creativity! Leadership Education in the classics and using the Seven Keys is the best way to start a truly creative education. Add to this your own initiative and the guidance of parents and mentors.

Thirteenth, dig deep and find your inner resiliency. Whatever happens, success goes to those who keep trying. After one great crisis season, Winston Churchill taught that the key to success is never to give up. He also said that courage is the most important virtue because without it the others aren't used.

Part of resiliency is to stay optimistic and enthusiastic in the face of whatever happens. Life is hard, and in 4th and 1st seasons it is harder than in the others; but that just means that we have more opportunity than ever to really help improve the world. Very little progress or positive change occurs during 2nd or 3rd seasons, but in times like these much can change very quickly. Of course, the change depends on leadership, which is why Leadership Education is so vital.

Fourteenth, and finally, grow your ambition! You were born to do great things, so don't settle for anything less.

Ambition sometimes gets a bad name, but that is mainly because it means different things in each of the seasons:

2nd: Personal Status

3rd: Personal wealth

4th: Making Sure the Right Side Wins

1st: Making Sure the Right Changes Happen

As you can see, even if great ambition were negative during 2nd or 3rd seasons, it is all positive during 4th and 1st seasons. For example, the American founding ambition to make sure the Colonies beat Britain is a great thing. Likewise the Northern ambition to end slavery in the Civil War and the Allied ambition to stop Hitler in World War II. Thank goodness for such high ambitions!

But the truly great ambitions came after these conflicts, in 1st seasons where the people set out to improve the world. Some of the changes were good, while others were bad. The difference was the quality of the leadership, based on the education of that generation's leaders.

In your generation, the world cries out for great change. So much needs to be fixed. So many things in this world today need to be improved.

This generation can do it. But like past generations, it will depend on the leadership of the next fifty years. And that will depend in large part on the education we get in the next five to ten years. Will you follow the old thinking of 3rd seasons and focus on career training? Will you accept mediocrity? If so, the future of freedom and prosperity will not be an improvement on what you inherited. If not, you need to learn right now, what the new rules of the 4th and 1st seasons are and become a master at them. Lead out in the new way of dealing with and solving challenges and crises and improving the world.

Make A Mark

What will be your mark on the world—improvement or further decline? It depends in large part on your education. It is up to you.

It is time for a generation to change the world, to drastically improve it. We believe it will be this generation that does it. Are we right?

We started this book by promising to tell it to you straight, to tell you the real deal. We have done that. The future depends on you. It doesn't get deeper or more real than that.

We also started with the thought that when God or the Universe wants to change the world, he sends a baby—perfectly timed to grow, learn, prepare and then take action at the right time. But there are times when one baby won't suffice, when the challenges facing the world are just too great, and so instead of a great reformer or a few key thinkers what is needed is a whole generation of leaders.

This happened in the Sixth Century B.C. and in the first decade of the Common Era, then again in the American Founding generation. George Washington, Benjamin Franklin, James Madison, Alexander Hamilton, Thomas Jefferson and so many more were part of this generation. In their youth, they worked to learn and get great Leadership Educations. Then, when the world needed them, they were ready.

It is happening again today. This is such a generation. But will you succeed? You get to decide. One thing is certain: to do so, you will need a superb, leadership, Thomas Jefferson-like education. In five years, you will either have the beginnings of such an education . . . or not. The ones who do will lead. Our challenge to you is to be one of them! It is who you were born to be. It is the Real, Genuine You. The world needs You.

8
ONE MORE THING!

Imagine yourself in the future—on the best day of your life! Close your eyes and picture it. Imagine how strong you are, how wise, how caring, compassionate and committed to good.

Young women often picture their wedding day, but not you. As wonderful as your wedding will hopefully be, it is not your best day. No, your best will come on the hardest day of your marriage, when you use your humility and wisdom to do the right thing—whatever it is.

Others picture the day their child is born, or when their child accomplishes some great thing. But that isn't it either. No, your best day will come in something very small and simple, like putting aside your busy projects and reading a story to a child when she asks. Do you have any idea how incredibly beautiful you will be on that day in that moment? How captivating and smart?

Without such days, the others—the ones that seem great—will never happen.

Young men sometimes picture a great victory on the athletic field, on the battlefield, in romance or in some great life achievement. But that will not be your best day. No, your best day will be a quiet day of contemplation and the hard-won but complete and total decision to dedicate your life to the right allegiance!

Some may envision honors, positions of authority, public accolades, riches, successes or fame. But the Real You knows that your best day will be spent playing with your children or grandchildren, listening quietly as they talk and giving wise counsel and later laughter during a walk in the woods, or on the beach, or while working together in the yard. Do you know how strong, successful, handsome and smart you will be that day? How truly awesome?

For those who are past your youth, that greatest day is still ahead! You were born to do miracles. You were born to change the world. But even more, you were born to love, to be happy, to enjoy this life journey. How much you enjoyed today is a good indication of how "on target" you are right now. But if you didn't enjoy today, don't look outside yourself or blame other people or circumstances. On the best day of your life, you'll know and live the truth that your happiness is entirely up to you—and controlled entirely by your thoughts and commitments, and nothing else.

Also, on your best day, your emphasis won't be on you—but rather on serving someone, helping somebody who really needs it, on really making a positive difference in someone's life. If you visualize yourself helping someone on your best day, and you notice the look in their eyes—really notice—you'll know why it's your best day.

YOUR BEST NOW

And here's the thing: If you think your best day is in the future, you're only partially right. Because on your best day you will live fully in the now, happily, today, in the present moment—which is the only place you feel happy and the time when you have the most power!

On your best day your heart and mind will be full of so much gratitude for the things you deeply and truly appreciate…

The world tries to convince everyone, and especially youth, that life is about ego, personal success, what others think of you, money, power or fame. All lies.

Instead of believing them, on your best day you will know and live these great and simple truths:

☛ Freedom is when you don't care how you look to others, who gets the credit for the good you do, or what others think of you;

but rather you focus on what is right and how you can help others feel happy…

☛ God/good is trying to get your attention right now and has some important things to tell you, so listen up…

☛ You don't have to know where you are going as long as you are following the right allegiance…

☛ You don't have to struggle and claw your way to the top because the *journey* is the main event. To love, serve, help, have fun and feel happy along the way are the whole point.…

☛ You don't have to set a timetable as long as you are doing the right things, because God/the Universe have it all worked out better than you ever could plan it anyway—so relax, keep doing your best, and smile a lot.…

And finally, you don't have to become great, because you already are. With that settled: What good can you do in the world?

What were you born to do with passion and great impact? Are you getting the education that will help you do it to your full potential? Are you wisely making the right choices as you learn the great lessons?

What was the "Real You" put on this earth *for*?

Whatever it is, you don't have to measure up to it in some way—you just have to do your best, and keep trying. Just never give up, and never give less than your best.

Even if you've done less than your best so far, it's never too late—start today. And if you're doing your best now, keep going and you will just naturally keep getting better.

THE BEST GENERATION

We have traveled all over this continent. We have met thousands and thousands of you. We know you well. Here's our prediction about you and your generation: We see in you the strength of Ernest

Shackleton, the compassion of Mother Teresa and the resilience of Abraham Lincoln. We see in you the dedication of Aung San Suu Kyi, the wisdom of Mahatma Gandhi and the humility of Benito Juarez. We see in you the potential of young George Washington and young Thomas Jefferson. We see eyes that have wept in the depths of misery and voices that have shouted to the rooftops for joy. We see leaders ahead who have paid the price to lead.

You are going to do great! You will pay the price of education, the price of service and the price of loyalty to family, spouse, children and freedom. You will lead in paying the price of humility and the price of conflict. Yes, we see the future being led by you.

As we've said so many times in the theme of this book: When God wants to greatly improve the world, He sends a baby. Whether you know it yet or not, He sent you!

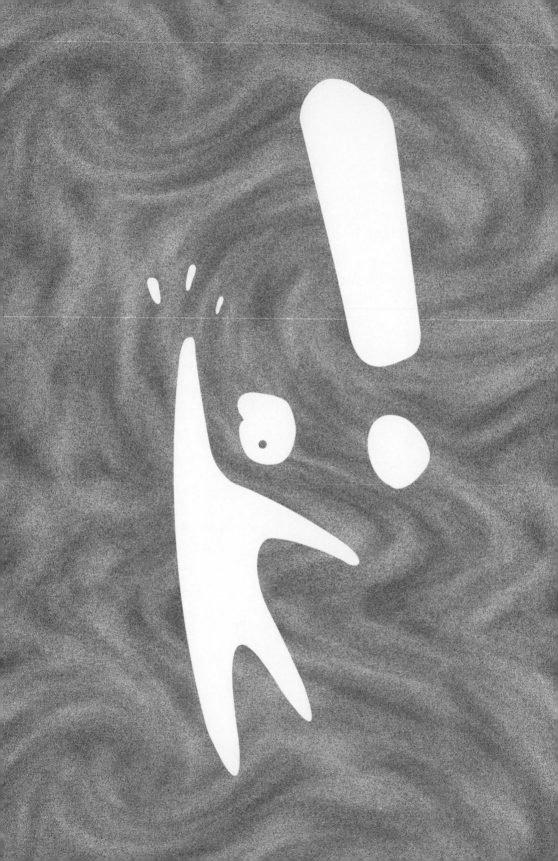

GENERAL

The original quote on God seeing the world's need and sending a baby comes from an unknown author.

The Jefferson quotes at the beginning of each chapter are taken from *Light and Liberty: Reflections on the Pursuit of Happiness*, words by Thomas Jefferson, edited by Eric S. Peterson. Quotes are sometimes spliced with other quotes.

The names and some details of stories have been changed to provide anonymity to those whose experiences are portrayed.

The authors used enallage (purposeful suspension of grammatical or other rules of writing) when they felt it would more effectively communicate with the audience or more clearly make a point.

Look for the books recommended on the Teen 100 and in these end notes at TJEd.org/purchase.

CHAPTER ONE

For further information on other concepts covered in this chapter, see the following:

Megatrends by John Naisbitt

Megatrends 2000 by John Naisbitt and Patricia Aburdene

Cashflow Quadrant by Robert Kiyosaki

The Jackrabbit Factor by Leslie Householder

A Whole New Mind by Daniel Pink

Revolutionary Wealth by Alvin Toffler

CHAPTER TWO

See more on concepts covered in this chapter from *A Thomas Jefferson Education* by Oliver DeMille, and *Leadership Education* by Oliver and Rachel DeMille.

A great read on the importance and power of the classics is *The Closing of the American Mind* by Allan Bloom.

The teen list is not the same as the college/adult list, which is found in the book *A Thomas Jefferson Education,* and at www.TJEd.org.

CHAPTER THREE

For details on and suggestions for types of mentors, see *The Student Whisperer* by Oliver DeMille and Tiffany Earl.

For more on mentoring from the Greek tradition, see *The Human Odyssey* by Thomas Armstrong. This book also teaches about the levels of human development, including the teen years and how they fit into a person's overall life progress.

For further information on other concepts covered in this chapter, see the following:

> *The Answer* by John Assaraf and Murray Smith
>
> *Leadership Education* by Oliver DeMille and Rachel DeMille
>
> *Launching a Leadership Revolution* by Chris Brady and Orrin Woodward

CHAPTER FOUR

See *The Real Thomas Jefferson* by Andrew Allison, et. al., for more information on Jefferson's love of learning.

Thanks to Neil Flinders for his mentoring on the concept of allegiance (taught in person to Oliver).

See *What Happy People Know* by Dan Baker for more on how fear hurts lives and how it can be overcome. For more on concepts about overcoming fear, see *The End of Fear* by Richard Schaub with Bonney Schaub.

For further information on other concepts covered in this chapter, see the following:

The Five Love Languages of Teenagers by Gary Chapman

Finding Ever After by Robert Paul

William Shakespeare, *Twelfth Night*, II, v, 156-159

CHAPTER FIVE

For further information on other concepts covered in this chapter, see the following:

The Closing of the American Mind by Allan Bloom

Cultural Literacy by E.D. Hirsch

Democracy in America by Alexis de Tocqueville

Leading Minds by Howard Gardner

Leadership Education by Oliver and Rachel DeMille

Future Shock by Alvin Toffler

Revolutionary Wealth by Alvin Toffler

The Bridge at Andau by James Michener

A Whole New Mind by Daniel Pink

Illiberal Education by Dinesh D'Souza

Killing the Spirit by Page Smith

Dumbing Us Down by John Taylor Gatto

The Dictionary of Cultural Literacy by E.D. Hirsch

CHAPTER SIX

See *The Five Love Languages of Teenagers* by Gary Chapman.

For more on the great questions pre-teens and teens naturally ask, see the writings of Charlotte Mason, John Holt, Wayne Dyer, Mel Levine, Michael Platt, and James Dobson.

See the writings and audio products of Gary Smalley, Mary Beth Jones, Caroline Myss, and others by searching personalities, personality types, archetypes, etc. online.

CHAPTER SEVEN

The Deaton quote is from *Ownership Spirit* by Dennis R. Deaton.

For further information on other concepts covered in this chapter, see the following:

The Fourth Turning and also *Millennials* by William Strauss and Neil Howe

Our Home by C.E. Sargent

Cash, Cars and College by Janine Bolon

The Jackrabbit Factor by Leslie Householder

Ownership Spirit by Dennis R. Deaton

Career Renegade by Jonathan Fields

Less by Marc Lesser

The Age of Miracles by Marianne Williamson

ONE MORE THING

For further information on other concepts covered in this chapter, see the following:

The Gift of Change by Marianne Williamson

The Four Agreements by Don Miguel Ruiz

Become a Better You by Joel Osteen

The Science of Getting Rich by Wallace Wattles

Remembering Wholeness by Carol Tuttle

Lives of the Noble Greeks and Romans by Plutarch

Meditations by Aurelius

APPENDICES

Simulations in the appendix are protected by copyright, as is the rest of this book. For usage permissions, please email contact@TJEd.org.

Simulations

Simulations are a powerful way to learn and a key part of Leadership Education.

Note that all scenarios provided hereafter are fictional.

If you aren't an adult, do not complete any of these simulations without the permission and support of your parent or guardian. Tell your parents when you are doing any of them, and be sure you have their permission on all the details.

There is no set order to these—do them as they appeal to you.

Simulation: The Beach

Go to the beach for a day. Use sunblock and all other safety precautions. Be sure you have full permission from your parent/guardian. Take whatever precautions you need for safety, and a backpack with a notebook and pencils in it.

For the entire day, just sit in the sand and stare at the ocean, listening to the wind and the waves. Once in a while take a break, walk in the sand, eat or drink, and then return to your seat; write in your notebook about yourself—whatever comes to mind.

Do this all day. This can be a powerful and life-changing experience. Note that much of the power will likely come toward the end when you are over all boredom. Simply rest and listen to your thoughts and write your ideas.

Alternate Locations: Hike to a mountain view area; settle in a forest, in a desert ravine or at a lake. Watch the changes the movement of the sun makes in the way things appear; listen to the sounds in the stillness.

SIMULATION: RECOGNIZING POWER FLOW

Attend a government event with your parent/guardian or other adult they approve. This could be a session of your state legislature, a city council or school board meeting, a zoning meeting or other government event.

Go early and watch the people as they arrive. What do they do? Ask yourself why they do what they do. Take notes.

When the event begins, don't participate. Just watch. Watch the power. Try to see who has it, and when and why it shifts. See if the speaker has it, or someone who is quiet. Just watch and try to see who has the power at any given moment. Learn to recognize it and watch it flow. Observe collaborations, alliances, rivalries and rifts. If you don't "get it" at first, don't worry. This can take a while.

Just sit and keep trying. Watch everything going on in the room, and keep asking, "Where is the power?"

When you recognize it, ask, "Why did the power go to them?"

Stay seated and watching until everyone else is done and leaves. Often you will see much power evident right before and/or right after an event.

Take a notebook and write your thoughts, questions and conclusions throughout this experience.

If you don't feel like you really understood this well, go back and repeat the same process again. You will probably be amazed by how much better you are at it the second and especially the third time.

This simulation gives you a valuable skill for life.

SIMULATION: BOOK PARTY

Choose a book you love and invite five friends to read it and then discuss it with you on a set date. Run this like a birthday party, with invitations, refreshments, etc.

In your invitations, give the group time between the invite and the book party to get, read and think about the book (usually 3-4 weeks).

Request an RSVP one week after sending the invitations, so you know who is coming and can invite others if needed.

Maybe include a reading challenge with target dates and small prizes for the winners.

Remind all participants of the party one week before it occurs, and confirm that they are attending.

Call them all the day before the party and remind them about it. Decide in advance with your fellow party planners what your policy for participation will be. Perhaps you'll determine that only those who've completed the reading should attend. Or maybe they can come but only participate in the discussion if they've completed the reading. You decide what type of party you want it to be.

Get refreshments prepared; or, if you have asked others to bring treats, make reminder calls.

Hold the event! Do not be disappointed if only a few or even just one person comes. Book parties are new to people, and sometimes they just skip them at the last minute. Actually, this happens a lot! Relax; just have fun with whomever came. The fewer there are, the more depth you can go into during the discussion.

If your turnout is sparse, just keep doing it until the word gets out. If you include others in the actual planning and follow-through, you can probably count on at least those to take part and be prepared! Be sure to have lots of fun with the one or few who do come, and they will tell others about it.

If the book has a movie made of it, like Narnia or Lord of the Rings, Little Women, Emma, Jane Eyre, Les Miserables, etc., you can make it a movie party and just have reading the book be optional. This will get you more people, and you can always call people at the last minute and invite them to come watch the movie. (Remember though, this is ultimately about reading books, so always try to get them to read the book along the way.)

For the discussion, prepare a list of 10-20 questions you think are most interesting about the book (and movie). But don't fixate on your list. In fact, start the discussion by having each person tell what one thing most interested him or her about the book. If nobody has much to say, start by sharing your first, most important question, telling what you thought about it, and asking what they think.

You can almost always spark discussion by asking, "What did you really dislike about the book?" or "Who was your favorite character?"

Only use your list of questions if needed.

For the first time, about 40 minutes is good, unless the people get excited and don't want to stop. After the first time you might want to just let the group decide.

This can be so much fun! Thousands of youth have done this in recent years, and it is very popular among most who have tried it!

Be sure to include your parent/guardian in all the planning and details, and have them attend and participate a little in the event. Make sure your parent or guardian (and those of the invitees) approves of the book you choose for the book party. A youth colloquium is not the place for books that challenge your participants' core values of standards.

SIMULATION: THE REAL LIBRARY!

Spend a full day at a college/university library. Take pencils and paper for taking notes. Start the day on one end or the bottom floor of the building, and walk through each section of books. Go down each row, and read the topics of each section.

When you see a topic that interests you, whether it is the first, second or tenth topic you see, stop and read all the titles in the section.

Set aside every book that looks interesting to you. When you get to about twenty books in your pile, sit at a table or desk and read through the table of contents of each. When you see a section that interests you, turn to that page and read and skim that section of the book.

When you finish all twenty books, return to reading the titles in the same section you just left. When you finish the section, having skimmed all of the books that really interest you, then keep walking down the rows of books until you find another topic of interest. Then repeat it all.

See how many sections you get through in a day. Keep track of how far you get in the library, and start at that point doing the same thing on another day. Eventually try to complete the whole library.

You will be amazed at how much you learn in just one day!

If you want to, you can of course check out books if you have a library card and take them home to read in more depth. But you already know how to do this! The simulation is learning how to do this in a library. Again, you will be amazed at how much you learn.

SIMULATION: CURRENT EVENTS

Do the same thing as the last simulation, but in the periodicals and magazines section of the library! This will teach you a great deal about current events, in all your areas of interest.

SIMULATION: WHAT'S COMING NEXT?

Do the same thing as the last two simulations, but in a big bookstore that provides chairs and reading areas for its customers. This will be very different from the library, and you will learn more about trends and what's ahead in each field of interest than you could from library books.

Be sure to listen to your inner voice on what you choose to spend time on. There can be subjects that may be intriguing but not right for this time. Again, your core values and standards should be a guiding light for interpreting what you learn, and for what you decide to spend time on.

SIMULATION: SHAKESPEARE

Get the LEMI student workbook entitled Shakespeare Conquest and read it and complete all the assignments and projects. This can be done alone or even better in a group.

SIMULATION: FREEDOM

Get the LEMI student workbook entitled Key of Liberty and read it and complete all the assignments and projects. This can be done alone or even better in a group.

SIMULATION: MONEY

Play the Cashflow game with 1-4 friends. Schedule at least four hours for this. Play repeatedly until you easily get out of the Rat Race each time.

SIMULATION: BUSINESS PLANNING

Write a business plan for a business you would like to do. Use online resources and books on business planning. Take your plan to the local SBA (Small Business Administration) and get feedback and ideas in order to refine the plan.

Take the upgraded plan to at least two banks and discuss it with the business loan officer.

SIMULATION: THE POLLYANNA GAME

Schedule a two-hour period to be where you won't get interrupted. You should choose a quiet place in your house, home, yard or other appropriate setting. Be sure your parents know where you are and what you are doing.

Set your alarm for two hours, and then ignore time until the alarm rings.

Now, write down everything you appreciate.

Include everything you appreciate from all aspects of your life. If you get stumped, look around and see what you appreciate from your surroundings. Include what you appreciate about your family. List topics at the top of a page and list everything you appreciate from that topic.

This is meat to go deep, so just write everything you think of that you appreciate. When you get tired of this and think you have written everything possible, just sit and ponder until more ideas come. Keep doing this for the entire two hours.

This will be a powerful and profound experience if you give it your full focus and time. Enjoy it!

SIMULATION: DEPTH

Do you want to get really deep? Pick a character from the book *Lives*, by Plutarch, and read what Plutarch says about him or her. Then brainstorm every lesson you can learn from this character that applies to your life.

For example, what things does this character do that you should do more often? What flaws does this character have that you want to avoid? Was the character happy? Why or why not? What can you learn from this? And so on.

SIMULATION: EVENT

Attend and participate in a Youth for Freedom (YFF) youth conference or event. This will be a powerful, life-improving experience.

SIMULATION: FOR REAL

To learn how to get involved in real projects that are making a difference around the world, see The Center for Social Leadership at www.thesocialleader.com.

SIMULATION: ORGANIZED GROUP

Attend an organized group simulation at Williamsburg Academy (www.wacademy.org) or elsewhere. This experience will be among the best in your youth, and nobody should miss this!

SIMULATION: ORGANIZE ONE YOURSELF

Help organize a group simulation in your area or online. As with all these simulations, get your parents' or guardian's help on this.

A number of simulations and scenarios, all fictional of course, are included on the TJEd for Teens Website (www.TJEdforTeens.com).

Go peruse this site and these simulations to get a feel for what's available.

Attend a Face-to-Face with Greatness seminar and learn more about how to do simulations (www.facetofacewithgreatness.com).

LEADERSHIP EDUCATION RESOURCES

TJEd.org
The official website of Thomas Jefferson Education.

Every person has inner genius. Thomas Jefferson Education consists of helping each student discover, develop and polish her genius. This is the essence and very definition of great education.

TJEd.org provides articles, videos and downloadable resources to help parents and teachers apply the 7 Keys of Great Teaching and the 4 Phases of Learning so your kids will love to learn, and you will inspire them and bring them face-to-face with greatness.

This Week in History
TWIH is a daily online resource that brings your home school or classroom to life! Whatever you want to learn, whatever there is to teach, it starts with history...

With a subscription to This Week in History, each day's resources are an adventure in math, science, language skills, geography, current events, the arts and so on – all tied to events in history. For just $9.99 per month, you have the world of learning available to help you lead and inspire your students to explore, learn and excel! The content is searchable by date, topic and key word, and subscribers can access the whole year's archive at any time.

Of all the things you'll spend $10 on each month, This Week in History is not only a great value, but a time saver and a worry eliminator. There's no better value in "curriculum" anywhere. Check out our Sample Week and User Reviews at: TJEd.org/TWIH

OTHER WORKS BY OLIVER DEMILLE

A Thomas Jefferson Education:
Teaching a Generation of Leaders for the 21st Century

Is American education preparing the future leaders our nation needs, or merely struggling to teach basic literacy and job skills? Without leadership education, are we settling for an inadequate system that delivers educational, industrial, governmental and societal mediocrity? *A Thomas Jefferson Education* presents a new educational vision based on proven methods that really work! Teachers, students, parents, educators, legislators, leaders and everyone who cares about America's future must read this compelling book.

Leadership Education: The Phases of Learning
(with Rachel DeMille)

This volume continues the Leadership Education Library with a survey of human development research that supports the TJEd philosophy and methodology, plus sections on each of the Phases of Learning: Core, Love of Learning, Transition to Scholar, Scholar and Depth. In addition, this book illuminates the adult phases of Mission and Impact, with a special Coda on Grandparenting. If you want to implement Leadership Education in your home, school, business or personal life, you will find this an invaluable tool. This inspirational book is considered by many to be the DeMille's best work.

A Thomas Jefferson Education Home Companion
(with Rachel DeMille and Diann Jeppson)

This handy sequel has practical suggestions for helping children progress toward and succeed in scholar phase, including adult skills acquisition, how to conduct a successful family reading time, mentoring tips, club organization helps, how to create a "Momschool", etc.

The Student Whisperer
(with Tiffany Earl)

This book is designed to help you become a great mentor—a true Student Whisperer and leader at the highest level. It will also help you work effectively with such mentors as you pursue your goals and life mission. This book is part deep teaching of the vital principles of great Leadership Education, part self-help workshop, part example through parables, and part exploration of the great ideas that make mentoring and quality learning most effective at all ages.

FreedomShift: 3 Choices to Reclaim America's Destiny

Americans who are so demonstrably willing to labor and sacrifice for the benefit of their posterity can only allow the destruction of the forms that protect our freedoms if they do not understand what freedom is, nor how to maintain it.

A FreedomShift is needed today; and to accomplish it, Oliver DeMille proposes The 3 Choices to Reclaim America's Destiny. Can it be possible that such a peaceful revolution can be accomplished by three simple choices made by a relative few?

The Coming Aristocracy

The Coming Aristocracy is a book for anyone concerned about the decline of America and the steady loss of freedom. Drawing from years of intense and exhaustive research, Oliver DeMille demonstrates why social, economic, and political equality are being steadily eroded. He highlights crucial constitutional changes, analyzes the current economic crisis, explains why both liberals and conservatives promote aristocracy, and articulates a formula for restoring the American republic.

AUDIOS

The Seven Keys of Great Teaching

"The 7 Keys of Great Teaching" is an mp3 audio download of a two-hour presentation delivered before a live audience by Oliver DeMille. One of the most popular and widely shared of our audios, this inspiring lecture covers the basics of TJEd:

- The 3 Types of Education
- The 4 Phases of Learning
- The 7 Keys of Great Teaching

Engaging, entertaining and informative, "The 7 Keys of Great Teaching" is an excellent first tool for sharing the principles and overview of Leadership Education with family, friends, educational advisers, mentors, spouses, students, etc.

Core and Love of Learning Seminar Highlights

"Core and Love of Learning: A Recipe for Success" is a 5-hour audio series consisting of highlights from a two-day seminar presented by Oliver and Rachel DeMille in 2007. This mp3 download will help you develop and expand your vision of how the TJEd model can work in your home. Oliver and Rachel's spontaneous, candid, intimate, touching, humorous and profound commentary on Leadership Education in the home includes:

- Daily and Weekly Scheduling
- Organizing Space in your home to support Thomas Jefferson Education
- What to simplify and what to beef up
- What to say "No" to, and when to say "Yes"

- Music and other lessons and how to best integrate them
- Which books work best for what ages
- Organizing a big family with students at different ages and Phases
- Separating discipline from academics
- Using outside activities without letting them take over
- Tips for making mornings work

The Four Lost American Ideals

In the hour-long recorded lecture, "The Four Lost American Ideals" Oliver DeMille draws from intensive study of the Founding generation to identify five defining ideals of Americanism: 1) Freedom, 2) Georgics, 3) Providence, 4) Liber and 5) Public Virtue. Although the first, Freedom, has not yet been fully lost, it is steadily declining because of the loss of the other four. These four ideals permeated early American society but have largely been forgotten.

The Freedom Crisis

Freedom lovers are losing, says DeMille, because they've been trained to think sensus solum. This type of thinking stifles creativity, inhibits innovation, creates cultural rigidity, and fails to sway the thinking populace. In order to conquer this ingrained challenge and win the battle for freedom, three things must occur: 1) Widespread Sensus Plenior, 2) Successful Innovators Building Effective Mini-Factories and 3) Statesmen & Stateswomen. Unless we can accomplish these goals, freedom will be lost for future generations. Absorb this 53-minute recorded speech to learn what these mean and how you can contribute to the solutions.